George Tuthill Borrett

Letters from Canada and the United States

George Tuthill Borrett

Letters from Canada and the United States

ISBN/EAN: 9783742863034

Manufactured in Europe, USA, Canada, Australia, Japa

Cover: Foto ©Thomas Meinert / pixelio.de

Manufactured and distributed by brebook publishing software
(www.brebook.com)

George Tuthill Borrett

Letters from Canada and the United States

LETTERS

FROM

CANADA

AND

THE UNITED STATES.

BY

GEORGE TUTHILL BORRETT, M.A.,

FELLOW OF KING'S COLLEGE, CAMBRIDGE.

LONDON:

PRINTED FOR PRIVATE CIRCULATION,

BY J. E. ADLARD, BARTHOLOMEW CLOSE.

———

1865.

PREFACE.

THE following letters were addressed to my father
upon the occasion of a three-months' tour through
Canada and the Northern States of America. Some
of my friends who have seen them in manuscript, and
others who have not, have kindly expressed a wish to
see them in a more legible form. If any apology be
needed for putting into print what was written with
no such object, this must be mine. With the exception of a few omissions of more private matters, and
some additions to the closing pages, which were chiefly
written on the voyage home, the letters remain in their
original state. To all who care to read a traveller's
first impressions of the country and people of which
it speaks I now offer this volume, in the hope that
its perusal may not unpleasantly occupy an occasional
half-hour.

GEO. T. BORRETT.

June, 1865.

I.

LIVERPOOL TO MONTREAL.

On board " The North American,"
Saturday, August 13th, 1864.

AFTER being knocked about for nine days and
nights on the open sea, we sighted land this morning
at twelve o'clock, and are now proceeding in compara-
tive quiet through the straits of Belle Isle, with 700
miles still between us and the longed-for harbour of
Quebec. I do not know that I have much to tell you
at present, for our voyage has been marked by no
particular incident beyond the ordinary occurrences of
a trip across the Atlantic by this route ; but it is such
a pleasure to find yourself in smooth water again—
not running your head into your neighbour's ribs, nor
breaking your shins against every bench in the saloon
—that, notwithstanding the fact that I could now
relieve my eyes, wearied as they are with straining
into empty space, by a view of land on each side of
our beam, I am seized with an almost involuntary
impulse to sit down at the table below, and communicate at once to you the joyful announcement that we

1

have said good-bye to the Atlantic and its troubles, and can now reckon with tolerable certainty upon a speedy completion of what the captain considers "a good passage."

Sea voyages, I suppose, are usually pretty much such as we have hitherto had, for I imagine that what I have seen enables me to form a good idea of an ordinary ocean trip, and I do not see that this idea is much different from my preconceived notions of such an excursion; and probably your notions of the same would very much coincide with mine, and so I shall not trouble you with any attempt at a lengthy description of so hackneyed a subject. "Nothing in the world to do, with plenty of time to do it in," to my mind, is the most brief and accurate description of a passenger's life on board ship; and I cannot see that a sailor's life, in such weather as we have had, is much more than an elaborate working out of the same satisfactory arrangement. Perhaps I am hard upon the seafaring race; possibly I am so constituted that I cannot extract from a continued contemplation of the "vasty deep" that mental and bodily exercise which land-lubbers like myself are taught to seek as necessary to salvation of soul and body. All I know is that I can imagine no life which I would not choose rather than a sailor's in good weather, when there seems to me to be such an absence of employment of hand or brain as no other occupation in the world would offer. Say what they will, sailors will never persuade me that life aboard can be anything but intolerably dull; poetise as they may, enthusiasts will never make me believe that the simple fact of dashing through the water at full speed can compensate for the lack of anything to see or do on the way. It seems to me that a sailor must depend, for the bare excitement which will keep the rust from his mind and muscle, upon the fury of the winds and waves; and if such be the only medium through which he can get that necessary amount of excitement, Heaven defend me from a life like his!

Now you must not imagine, from these few observations, that we have been gliding along as it were upon a mill-pond, with a fair breeze all our way. We have had, as I remarked above, "a good passage," yet that by no means signifies a smooth one. In fact, I have observed by experience that this is a nautical expression of wonderful elasticity, which, in the mouths of a captain and his crew, may mean anything short of actual shipwreck. But we had two days, about half way across the Atlantic, which, compared with the other days, were enjoyable; still, even then, I think we all found it very hard to contrive some species of amusement. We stared at the water, and vowed it was beautiful; we stared at the sky (for it was the only time when it was visible), and declared it to be clearer than it was at home; and for a time, no doubt, the

contemplation of the sea and sky, under such favorable circumstances, is very pleasant; but, like venison every day for dinner, it grows stale; and, after all, if the eye is to rest on no sign of animal or vegetable life, the solitudes of nature, to please the ordinary observer, must be of a far more imposing character than that which is presented by the ocean on a calm day. And so I thought with myself, as I sat upon the deck for several consecutive days, and strained my eyes in every direction, in the hope of seeing a porpoise at least, or a gull, or a distant sail—anything, in fact, to convince me that I had a companion in life, if it had been only a wild goose. And then I wished it would blow a gale, or that somebody would go up a mast and tumble off, or that it would rain, or snow, or freeze, or do anything but preserve the imperturbable calm, which provoked me with its excessive dulness. And yet, I suppose, rough thick weather must be admitted to be duller still. Yet there is this consolation, perhaps, though but a poor one, that in a fog you may possibly comfort yourself with the idea that there *might* be something to see if it was only clear, while in clear weather you see only too clearly that there is absolutely nothing to see at all; but, at the same time, there is a great deal of sameness and monotony about a damp fog, and more about a well-sustained, heavy roll in an Atlantic swell; and the fun of seeing the soup in your lap, and your neighbour's fork within an ace of your

eye, soon becomes a sort of practical joke which the Second Life Guards would hardly perpetrate; and I am afraid you would, as I did, inevitably come to the conclusion that an ocean voyage, rough or smooth, is particularly dull.

These are my general impressions, the result of what little experience I have had; but do not suppose that I have found this voyage very tedious or wearisome. Luckily, we have a better selection of passengers than the first sight of them led me to anticipate, and we have some of us fraternised wonderfully together; and the effect of our growing intimacy has been to let out some curious revelations, which have kept our tongues alive, and our ears on the alert, through many an hour of our long journey. But if I am to introduce you to the inmates of the ship, I think I ought to begin with the captain. Well, the captain is a remarkably pleasant, affable man, who entertains us at the table with good anecdotes of his nautical experience, and, what is far more to his credit, manifests an amount of caution and skill in the conduct of the ship, which the late officers of this company never displayed; for I cannot but see that this route is a very dangerous one, and nothing but extreme care can guide a vessel safely through the perils of the northern fogs and icebergs; and the knowledge that this company has lost no less than eight steamships in as many years makes us appreciate the more highly the presence of these estim-

able qualities in our present captain.   Next to him
sits a gushing young damsel of three-and-twenty, who
is going out to be married under the escort of a Canadian parson, who occupies the seat on her left, and
manifests the most affectionate zeal in his delicate
office.   On the other side of the captain sits an elderly
Englishman, who has travelled throughout the length
and breadth of the New World, and has been very
kind in putting me up to everything that ought to be
seen, and how to see it.   My place is between him
and an agreeable young English banker, with whom I
shall probably travel as far as Toronto, and in whom
I expect to find a very pleasant *compagnon de voyage;*
and on the other side of the table sit two young limbs
of the law from Lincoln's Inn, on a long-vacation tour,
like myself; and opposite them a Canadian doctor, who
is delightfully vulgar and amusing.

These are the passengers with whom I have chiefly
fraternised; but lower down the table is a wonderful
specimen of what most of us at first supposed to be a
member of the swell mob.   But by this gentleman
hangs a tale, for we had observed a strange desire
evinced by this personage to watch the movements of
a repulsive-looking individual, with very long dirty-
black hair, whose features indicated unmistakable
felony; and inquiry into the matter has revealed to
us the somewhat startling fact that the long-haired
miscreant is no more nor less than his face foretold—

that he is, in fact, a felon who has been captured in London, and is now on his way to Quebec, in charge of the flash cockney, who is a well-known serjeant in the London detective force. As you may suppose, this discovery was not particularly well received in the saloon, more especially amongst the ladies, with whom the assurance that the prisoner was locked up in his cabin at night did not seem to compensate for the disagreeable associations attached to the idea of sitting at table with him throughout the day. We had hardly acquainted ourselves with the truth of this story, when a rumour spread amongst the passengers that there was another individual on board whom it was found necessary to lock up in his cabin; and true enough we discovered it to be that there was a wretched man below who had come on board dead drunk, and had kept so ever since, and had lately been seized with a severe attack of delirium tremens, which made him so violent as to render it imperative that he should be tied down in his berth. So this was another subject of conversation, and everybody wondered what the miserable creature would be like, if he ever recovered from his attack, and had the face to show in the saloon, and was uncommonly disappointed to find, on his first appearance yesterday at the table, that he was, after all, when sober, an extremely quiet, well-behaved gentleman, with a very agreeable wife and daughter, who were evidently well used to the fellow's eccentricities.

The rest of our table, and that on the other side of the saloon, are filled up with Scotch and Irish, mostly of the timber-merchant class, and several French Canadians; and amongst them is a Yankee captain, in whom I have been immensely disappointed, for he is one of the most agreeable of the passengers, and I feel sure that if I meet many more such specimens of the Yankee race, my prejudices against them will be completely smothered; and from what I hear on board this vessel, I should not wonder if that were the result of my visit to their country. At any rate, I am pretty certain that I shall not find them such a set of ruffians as I anticipated; indeed, I am positive that no branch of the human race could present such a miserable picture as that which I had painted to myself as the portrait of a Yankee; so they cannot lose in my estimation, and must, as far as I see, gain. The junior officers of the ship are a decent lot of men; and the steerage passengers, though not very sweet, are not noisy; and here I think you have a miniature view, which will enable you to form some idea of the society on board our gallant ship.

And now, having given you this slight sketch of the vessel and her freight, I suppose I ought to try and say a few words about the voyage itself; but, as I said before, an ocean voyage is characterised by no incident whatever unless you have a gale, and fortunately for our peace and comfort we were not so favoured.　To begin with, then, our first three days, after leaving Londonderry, were days of but little progress, for we had a head wind and a heavy sea; and glad though I may honestly say I was to make acquaintance with the waves of the Atlantic, I may quite as honestly say that I have no anxiety to cultivate this acquaintance, or be anything more than a very distant friend. I should like to give you some idea of the " swell" on the Atlantic, but am afraid that you would be disinclined to believe in the justice of my comparison, if I were to suggest to you anything on land with which to compare it; yet I think I may venture thus far with safety, and say that the rising and sinking upon the ocean swell is more like going up and down Holborn Hill than anything of which I can just now think; by which I mean that if you could fancy yourself gliding down such an inclined plane as that of Holborn Hill, and up such another as Snow Hill, with a long heavy lurch on to one beam as you went up, and another perhaps longer and heavier on to the other beam as you came down, and then imagined this grand but stomach-trying movement to continue for several days without cessation, you would get some notion of the kind of thing to which we had to get accustomed.

Dinner, under these circumstances, is, naturally enough, a matter of some little difficulty. The first two days I was rather seedy, and showed but little desire for eating or drinking, but still I was not so

unhappy as many. The fact is that I can stand the
upward and downward movement tolerably well; but
it is the complex motion of the pitch and the roll that
to the uninitiated is so heartrending. However, the
third day saw me at the table with a famous appetite,
and this, I believe, lasted me throughout the voyage;
and it really is wonderful to see how readily one can
adapt one's self to the vicissitudes of fortune, or rather
of the ship; but still I do not consider that I have yet
mastered the difficulty of taking soup in a heavy sea.
The plates and dishes are, of course, all secured between layers or ledges of iron running parallel with the
edges of the table; and this necessary but curious
arrangement suggests the idea of pigs feeding out of a
trough; and very much like pigs many of us fed, for
there was, as there is on the Peninsula and Oriental
steamers—as there always is, I believe, on any passenger steamers—a profusion of viands of every kind;
indeed, many of the dishes each day have been quite
first-rate, insomuch so, that I find great difficulty in
appreciating the ignominy of position attached to the
status of "son of a sea-cook," and fancy that I should
not much object to being looked upon as the offspring
of such a *chef* as had the superintendence of our
cuisine.

On Sunday, the roughest day perhaps of all, we had
a somewhat poor attempt at service, in the prayers and
psalms whereof the motion of the vessel gave us much

the appearance of the United States " Jumpers" and
" Shakers ;" while in the sermon the Canadian parson
was both mentally and bodily emphatically at sea. The
next two days were finer and more enjoyable, and our
log-book showed a much higher score of miles completed in the day's run. Wednesday, again, was rough;
Thursday pretty much the same; Friday cold and
foggy. And now I began to see the dangers and
difficulties of this route; for we were fast approaching
the track of the icebergs in their passage from the
North to the Gulf-stream, in whose genial warmth
they are gradually dissolved, after spreading around
them, in their course from the Arctic regions, an
amount of cold and fog which must be felt and seen
to be believed. And here it was that the captain evi-
denced those estimable qualities to which I have alluded
above. Nothing could exceed the cautious vigilance
with which he superintended the steering of the ship.
The fog was at times awfully thick, and the air so excessively cold, that though we could not discern the
ice, we felt pretty sure that it was all around us. The
vessel was put at half speed, with sails furled; but the
sea was high and the wind aft, and so a collision at
the rate at which even then we were going would have
been most disastrous. The excitement of this situation, however, did not last long, and Friday night was
clear enough to enable us to resume our usual speed.
But it was bitterly cold, and all my means of wrap-

ping up did little towards keeping the damp out of my bones.

I do not know that I was more surprised with anything on the voyage than this excessive cold. It appears to be caused by the ice which drifts down from the North, from Greenland and Labrador, and the vast area of cold water with which these icebergs travel; and the fogs are created by the meeting of these cold waters of the Northern seas with the warm waters of the Gulf-stream, and the condensation of the hot air from the South as it flows over the cold waters from the North. This I imagine to be the true explanation of these extraordinary cold fogs, which have baffled the art of every navigator; but whatever it may be, it undoubtedly is a striking characteristic of this route, and by no means an agreeable one. I had no idea, when I left Liverpool, that I was about to be brought into such a freezing climate; in fact, it never struck me that I was about to visit the neighbourhood of Greenland; but a little reflection enabled me to see that our going so far north is only the result of the *curve* which we must necessarily take in order to get by the shortest route from one to another of two points situated as Liverpool and Quebec in the upper part of the Northern Hemisphere. I am afraid that I cannot exactly explain what I mean by this " curve;" but I think you will see it by taking an orange and laying it on either end upon the table, and you will find that, to take the *shortest* line from one to another of two points, each situated near the top of the orange, you will have to ascend slightly to that part where the circumference is smaller, and in coming down again to the point of your destination you will complete a portion of a curve, which, on a larger scale upon the earth's surface, is called in navigation "the great curve." It is thus, then, that this route brings those who take it into such high latitudes. Of course, the Belle Isle line is only open to navigation in the height of summer; but even now, as I have said, the thermometer stood so low, that I might easily have imagined myself to be in the depth of a severe winter.

This morning was clear and sunny, though the air was still sharp; but the mists were all gone, and now for the first time I got a view of the icebergs which had been our constant terror yesterday. They are certainly of a most imposing character, and with the sun shining brightly upon their jagged and broken edges, present an appearance upon the surface of the ocean of which I can give you no idea. They are of almost every hue and shape—some like fantastic castles with marble turrets and dark-shadowed casements; some like gigantic conical ant-hills; some like cathedral spires; others like Eastern mosques with rounded domes; all a strange jumble of hard edges and grotesque outlines, which assume a thousand different forms as the vessel speeds by their lofty sides, and brings their various peaks, at each yard of her progress, into a new alignment with the eye. Then there were whales spouting all round them, and porpoises rolling, and gulls and divers upon the waves, and, best of all, land in sight (though not to my inexperienced eyes till long after the sailors had descried it) ; and so this morning has passed away pleasantly enough, and my appetite has gone up a dozen degrees; in fact, I feel myself another man altogether, and quite agree with the Irish sailor, who vowed that, after all, the best part of going to sea was the getting to land again.

Monday, August 15th.

Our voyage is now pretty nearly closed; we have our pilot on board and are steaming up the St. Lawrence with a fair wind, and by breakfast time to-morrow morning shall be (we hope) off the Citadel of Quebec. Sunday was a splendid day, and though not a very smooth one, for a screw steamer *will* roll, yet a favorable one for the log-book tale, for it gave us a run of nearly 300 miles in the twenty-four hours, which was more than the captain thought the ship " had in her." Icebergs were still plentiful up to a late hour on Saturday evening, but most of them were rendered harmless by having drifted ashore on Belle Isle, or Newfoundland, where the waves broke over them grandly. Once we counted twenty-three in view, some of course diminutive, but many of enormous dimensions, 150 or 200 feet above the water, and many hundred yards in breadth and length. Such a height above the level of the water gives an enormous sum total of cubic feet, for you must remember that floating ice carries *eight* times as much of its mass below the water as is visible above. Some huge monsters had stranded in water where the chart showed a depth of many fathoms.

I dare say you have not a very intimate acquaintance with the geography of these inhospitable regions. I was very shaky on the subject, but am decidedly improving. The straits of Belle Isle lie between the coast of Labrador and Newfoundland, and the island whence they take their name is at the entrance to the straits. It is a bleak barren rock, enveloped in fog, and snow, and ice, and perhaps you cannot quite see why it bears so promising a name. Some of the passengers suggested that it was a very poor joke on the part of some sarcastic navigator; but I can easily suppose the most uninviting of rocks to be welcomed as "beautiful" by any sailor who had been long knocked about in those dreary waters. The straits are about thirty miles wide on the average, and a hundred miles in length, but there is a strong current through them which carried us along at an immense speed: and now we are safe across the gulf of the St. Lawrence, and 600 miles from the Atlantic, in water as clear and smooth as glass, with fine scenery on either side of us, and a bright blue sky above.

It is a wonderful river, the St. Lawrence, far more like a large inland sea than what you or I are accustomed to look upon as a river. For several hundred miles from the ocean its banks are barely visible, and where they can be seen in this clear atmosphere would be quite invisible under our English sky, and even now at this great distance up the stream, over 600 miles, the width of the river is at times as much as thirty. But, of course, this marvellous display of natural irrigation is the great wonder of every stranger, and had I not been in the South of Europe I should have been as much astonished with the extraordinary clearness of the atmosphere. There is at this moment in sight a rock and signal station eighty miles distant from the spot where we now are. Such a statement will hardly be believed at home, but the outline is as definitely marked as if it were within ten miles. We are now in a very different climate, in fact it is fast becoming uncommonly hot, and after the cold through which we have passed the heat tells upon us with tenfold effect. I do not think I found it so warm in the Mediterranean last month, and I am sure I did not see what has been amusing us more or less all the afternoon, "the mirage" and its quaint impositions of distant lakes and inverted mountains. Sometimes the whole of the hills on each side of us were seen repeated topsy-turvy on the horizon : all the ships were double, that is, had an inverted image of themselves above them; one in the far distance had a third reflection of itself standing on the hull of the inverted image— this appearance, I believe, is very unusual—and still further from us was seen hanging in the air the image of a vessel which was " hull down " below the horizon, totally out of sight. This last certainly is a most extraordinary instance of the atmospherical refraction which creates the morning and evening twilight, and brings most forcibly to one's mind the means by which we are enabled to see the sun's disc so much earlier and later than it would, but for this refraction, be visible. The others are curious instances of seeing double; from which, however, I do not wish you to infer, that to see things in this way it is at all necessary to go through the same preliminaries as are indispensable to the attainment of the same result at home.

10 p.m.—We have all been on deck gazing in wonder at the Aurora Borealis, as it has for the last hour and a half been darting up its roseate streaks of fire from the northern horizon. The moon is shining with a brightness which I have only seen equalled at Malta, but her rays seem to have little or no effect in diminishing the powerful light of the Aurora. I wonder why this is not more often seen at home. It is visible any fine night in Canada, far further south than England.

QUEBEC,
Wednesday, August 17th.

I am now safe and snug at Russell's Hotel, Quebec. We reached the custom-house wharf at 7 a.m. yesterday, and may consider that we have made a good passage, having accomplished the distance of something under 3000 miles in less than eleven days. Every one was up very early yesterday morning to see the scenery of the St. Lawrence and the view of the city as we approached. The banks had contracted very much since we saw them the day before, and the stream was studded with numerous islands, uncultivated but prettily wooded, till just as we reached Quebec the river narrowed to the very respectable, but for this continent insignificant, width of *two* miles. The banks all along were thickly populated; French farms and country villages alternated on either side; neat looking villages with pretty churches fringed the margin of the water, and shoals of little fishing boats plied their trade along the shores.

Seven o'clock had just struck when we breasted the citadel of Quebec, and fired an imposing salute from two little pocket guns on the main deck. Quebec is grand from the river, clustering at the foot of a bold precipice from which the citadel frowns down upon the stream, and round behind the citadel walls creeping up the back of the rock with picturesque roofs and tower-

ing spires, which glitter in the sunlight like crystal.
The cause of this peculiar brilliancy is the fact that
the material used for roofing is tin. All the best
houses, all church spires, all domes and gable ends are
covered with tin. In our climate of course this covering would barely last out a week; but here, where the
air is so perfectly dry, that corroding and rust are
almost unknown, tin, though the most expensive at
first, is in the end the cheapest as well as the most
durable metal for the purpose. It looks well, especially in the sun's rays; gives a good finish to the stone
buildings, and I have no doubt gathers less snow than
the old-fashioned slates and tiles. At any rate it is a
great addition to the scenery. Down below the town
and round the base of the rock are spacious quays, with
water deep enough to allow the largest vessels to lie
alongside; and across the stream on the opposite bank
is a fine range of hills, with a large town facing the
citadel, and known by the name of Levi Point—pronounced by Canadians Pint Leavy.

Breakfast over at our hotel, in company with some
of our passengers we hired a calèche, or rather a
couple of those peculiar vehicles, each of which carries
two persons. They are the funniest-looking machines,
with the oddest horses, that I have seen for a long
time; there is no pretence to strength or ornament
about them; two wheels with a diminutive imitation
of the London man-about-town's cab perched upon

them, and a little box-seat in front ; no springs, and a
horse all harness——and the vehicle is complete.   But
the horse can go ahead, like the population, and the
apparent absence of springs is possibly due to the indifferent pavement of the streets, which is in many of
them of wooden planks laid transversely across the
road, and in others of stone, so unevenly put down
that I think it really the worse of the two.   But the
streets are too steep to admit of the construction of a
good road, being for the most part narrow and tortuous, twisting in and out amongst the French-looking
houses of the " habitans " which throw out all sorts
of odd angles in every conceivable direction as if desi-
rous of thrusting in the way of a good street every
obstruction they possibly can.   From the strong de-
clivities on either side of the citadel heights I should
think there must be little need of sanitary regulations,
as the first heavy shower pours down a flood from
above which washes down, with the speed of a torrent,
all filth that would otherwise accumulate.   The upper
town is handsome and elegant——a striking contrast to
the lower ; but, after all, the city is one which does not
improve upon acquaintance; it looks extremely well
from the river, but will not do at all when you come
to examine it closely.   From the top of the citadel we
had a glorious view of the city, the river, and the surrounding country.   We strolled along the fortifications,
looked at the spot where Wolfe fell, heard the noon-

day gun fired from the summit of the fort, and the grand reverberation, caused by its discharge, amongst the opposite heights, and driving through the city proceeded to the celebrated falls of Montmorenci, by a pretty drive of ten miles along the northern bank of the river. These falls pleased us all immensely. They are far finer than anything of the kind I had seen in Europe. The body of water is enormous, the precipice over which it is dashed is 250 feet high, and the scenery above and below the falls romantic; all necessary adjuncts to a good waterfall.

MONTREAL,
Friday, August 19*th.*

A walk on the Esplanade, a lounge on the Terrace, a visit to the quays and the Houses of Parliament (a temporary erection while the buildings at Ottawa are in progress) finished my stay in Quebec, and in the afternoon my friend the banker and myself took the steamer for Montreal, where we are now located in the great hotel known as the St. Lawrence Hall.

This was my first introduction to the river steamers of the New World, and truly they are an institution to which nothing that we have can for a moment be compared for comfort and speed combined. The American river-boat, of which the Canadian is a copy, is nothing more nor less than an immense floating hotel, a characteristic type of the people themselves, a curious combination of democratic follies and aristocratic propensities ; a mixture of every kind of life—fast life, slow life, busy life, and lazy life, all under one roof.   The saloon is a fine handsome room of great length and good height, fitted up with exaggerated decorations, extravagant and, as *I* think, tasteless.   Along either side are the state cabins, each and all a good bedroom in itself, comfortably arranged and extremely well ventilated ; and around them, on the outside, runs a sort of open deck or platform, where the passengers sit and promenade at their pleasure.   At 6 p.m. was served in the saloon, at the lower end, which is set apart as a dining-room, a handsome " high tea ;" and after tea there was music, cards, chess, and so on, till late in the evening, when, after a final moonlight walk outside, the passengers turned in.   I found my bed very comfortable, so did my companion, in so much so that we both had great difficulty in rousing ourselves on reaching Montreal, where we arrived in the morning at 7.30.

I am extremely glad that I came by boat rather than by rail, contrary to the advice of some of my friends ; for, though the journey occupies more time, yet the boats are very fast, the river is worth seeing, and the little insight I have gained into the American river-boat life has well repaid me for the extra time thus occupied.   Besides, it is cheap travelling, and very amusing. I know (at *present*, at least) no other place where you can see a working artisan in fustian sitting down at table next a well-dressed lady, and lounging on an elegant sofa side by side with a high-bred swell. And then there is such a delightful air of perfect independence and absence of respect for anything or anybody, an amount of self possession which is quite charming; and yet a certain civility withal, but rude and unpolished, as I should hardly have expected it in a district where the population is considerably more than half of it of French extraction. I never recollect seeing such an example of the great principle of self-help as was displayed to me that evening at tea, where every one, not bearishly or greedily, but with cool deliberate self-possession, helped himself or herself to the dish which was nearest, without a thought for the want of other appetites. I do not mean to say that there is any lack of charity amongst the Canadians; from what I hear I believe no people can be more kind, attentive, and hospitable; but the great idea amongst them all seems to be "help yourself," "never do for another what he can do for himself," good maxims enough in their way, but here, I suspect, carried a stretch too far. Fashion seems to be set by the lower classes, though that, of course, is a term which would not be heard in a country like this, "where every man is as good as his neighbour, and, if anything, better." Manners are taken from the same class. No waiter addresses you

as " Sir ;" no cabman, or porter, or crossing sweeper
(if there be any), would dignify you with such
a title.   Why should he ?   He is away from the
stuck-up one-horse aristocracy of England ; he looks
upon them with pity and contempt, calls them " proud
and poor," "ten generations behind the age,"
" worthy only of a glass case and a place in a museum
of antique curiosities."   He is, in fact, un-English ; he
tells you that he is not, but he *is*, a Yankee—a Yankee
in the sense in which we use the term at home, as
synonymous with everything that smacks of democracy.
You may accuse him of a desire for annexation to the
Northern States of America, but he will be so
loud in denying it, that you will have to change the
subject.   You may take up the key note of the
' Times,' and charge him with want of loyalty to the
British Government, and he will of course as loudly
deny this ; but talk to him and you will see that independence is the " acme " of his desires, and to perfect
it he knows no other means than by " throwing off the
British yoke."   The day of final emancipation from
the apron-strings of the mother country may not be yet
at hand, but the child is fully weaned, and the novel
scheme for a grand confederation of the British provinces of this continent, which is now being broached
in the journals, shows that he is shortly intending to
essay running alone.

We have taken a walk round Montreal, and are

greatly astonished with what we have seen. To people arriving with the idea of finding the inhabitants dwelling in log shanties and brushwood huts it must be a surprising sight to come upon a fine handsome city, with splendid buildings and noble churches, and all the indications of affluence which are characteristic of a wealthy commercial city; but of this I must speak in my next.

II.

MONTREAL TO TORONTO.

Montreal,
August 20th.

My last letter left me safely landed in Montreal, after a pleasant night-journey by steamer from Quebec, and gave you a hint, I believe, that this city far surpassed all my preconceived ideas of Canada. As yet, of course, I have only seen the more civilized side of Canadian life, and never expected to come across the rougher experiences of the Western forests in the streets of Montreal and Quebec; but I must fairly admit that I did not look for much that is grand, or costly, or imposing, or is associated with our ideas of wealth and luxury—I might almost say extravagance. Rapid development, brilliant progress, I knew I was sure to find, but not such a finished exterior. I anticipated a young colony with an old head, but not one with so old a face. Now my first walk through the streets of this city quite upset all my ideas, and showed me that there was much more of the Old World's architectural magnificence here than I had been willing to believe. Whether it was that my long-acquired habit of associating all capitals of agricultural districts with Ipswich prevented me from anticipating in this country any higher style of architecture than is to be met with in that most respectable but seedy town, I know not; but I certainly never expected to find that Canada had its Paris. However, I have been undeceived; and if you know any one labouring under a like delusion, you may at once enlighten them, and tell them that the buildings of Montreal surpass those of many a fine city on their side of the Atlantic.

The St. Lawrence Hall, the hotel in which I am staying—a well-known house amongst Canadians and Americans—is situated in the centre of the handsome edifices to which I have alluded. I will not trouble you with an enumeration of them, but merely say that these buildings are chiefly banks, offices of insurance, and other public companies, fine churches and chapels, spacious colleges, and asylums and hospitals, all well placed in broad streets, or detached in commanding positions. Those which pleased me most were the French cathedral, the Palais de Justice, and the Post Office—all perfect in their way. And then there are markets, three in number, and splendid stores, after the style of Cannon Street, and handsome squares in the suburbs, and grand wharves along the river, and much more that is worth a visit, of which I have not time to tell. The city is backed by a thickly-wooded mountain, round the summit of which I had a beautiful drive to get a view of the neighbourhood; and a grand one it is, with the city and its sparkling tin roofs beneath you, and the mighty St. Lawrence, *two miles wide*, beyond and all around the island on which the city stands, and at the western end of the city the far-famed Victoria tubular bridge spanning the breadth of the great river, and in the distance across the stream the purple mountains of Vermont, from which the Yankee sentinel can daily whet his hungry appetite by gazing at the tempting bait below. The 'New York Herald' is still at the old game, thirsting for " Canada's blood ;" and if I am to believe what I hear of the vast circulation and influence of that beautiful journal, there must be an enormous number across the frontier who are intent upon thus satiating their thirst. But Canada is quite deaf to all their threats, perfectly indifferent to their taunts and sneers; and yet I do not like to think that the 'Times' was right in its charges against the colony, and that the Canadian self-confidence is so much like apathy. They tell me that the volunteer movement is progressing, but I cannot say that I have seen anything of it yet. I only know that the volunteer department is entrusted to the care of the Attorney-general, under whose tender guidance it is said to thrive; from which fact I am led to conclude that lawyers here eschew red tape, else I should hardly expect to find a precocious young colony, of very liberal views and independent principles, consigning its military organization to such a wholesale dealer in that repulsive article.

The carriage in which my drive was taken, in company with a lady and gentleman whose acquaintance I have made, was a perfect model of what a *voiture à deux chevaux* should be, set upon large and light American wheels, and drawn by two excellent animals. There is, perhaps, more ornament upon the body of the carriage than we in England should admit, in the shape of electro-plated hinges, decorations, and devices; but extravagant ornament is the fashion here; and after all, I doubt whether we at home are not too sparing with our colours, in our endeavours to attain a tame neatness. I cannot understand why we consider it necessary at home to plant our carriages upon ponderous wheels, only suitable for Pickford's vans or the cars of the Indian Juggernaut, while here every vehicle but those adapted for the transport of the very heaviest goods is set on high, light, elegant wheels, that seem to run as if they could not help it, and carry the horses on before them, as the sleighs do in the snow. It is not that our English roads are too rough for the American wheels; Heaven knows, the turnpikes are bad enough in all conscience here. It is not, I feel sure, that, as a Yankee suggested to me, these light wheels would succumb beneath the weight of an English belle (it would take half-a-dozen Yankee belles to make a shadow). It *must* be, I suppose, as an irritated Englishman remarked, that an "old-country" horse would always be running away with them; and I verily believe that the adoption of these wheels is in no small degree due to the poverty of the horse-flesh of this continent. Still, "any-way," as the Yankees say, here are the wheels, and here, too, as I have already seen, are many and many an ingenious adaptation or improvement of a familiar old-world article, some easy method of working an old and elaborate contrivance, some simple modification of a complicated machine, some smart creation of American ingenuity; and that not only in the cities and towns, but even in the villages, the hamlets, the very fields—displayed alike in the gigantic grain-elevators of the corn-marts of the Western cities, and in the simple Canadian cottage pump; so that I begin to wonder no longer at the "mean," "pitiable," "paltry" position which we, the "poor old one-horse nation," occupy in the eyes of this enlightened "go-ahead" continent.

I suppose you will expect me to tell you something about the hotel life of the New World; and though I have not at present seen that peculiar characteristic of this continent in its fullest force and vigour, and shall not till I leave Canada, yet I am told that the St. Lawrence Hall, of Montreal, is intended to give, and

does give, an excellent miniature portrait of the vast
hotels of New York. You have read Sala's letters to
the 'Daily Telegraph,' and Russell's to the 'Times,'
and other works upon this subject, of which all of us
in England have heard so much. Some of them are,
of course, exaggerated; but it is difficult to convey a
powerful impression of anything in language which
shall be forcible but not extravagant; still, most of what
I had heard and read of this life is faithful and true,
and, accordingly, I looked in the St. Lawrence Hall for
just what I found, and little more. Well, I must ask
you to imagine a fine handsome house, after the style
of the new hotels in London or Paris, with a noble
entrance-hall, fronted by a covered arcade, opening
upon a wide well-built street. Before the doorway of
the hall will be a busy medley of carts, cabs, carriages,
and omnibuses in the road, and drivers, porters, passengers, and baggage on the pavement. Inside the
door, upon the right, is the reading-room, with the
journals in frames upon reading-desks along the walls;
and upon the left you will find the bar or coffee-room
—a sort of well-dressed English taproom—and all
about the doorway, the reading-room, and the bar, you
will jostle against a crowd of noisy visitors, and hear
such a buzz of human voices, as will drown the turmoil of the traffic in the street. A few steps further
in, and you will find yourself in a lofty second or inner
hall, where the noise and bustle seems ten times greater

than at the entrance to the hotel. Opposite to you,
at the further end of this inner hall, will be a long
counter, on which lies the visitors' book, with guide-
books, maps, almanacks, and directories, and behind
the counter you will see the *maître-d'hôtel*, with his
cashiers, clerks, and various assistants. On the right
of the hall you will find the post office and newspaper-
stall, circulating library, and telegraph bureau; and on
the left the lavatory and, not the least important, the
barber's shop. All along the counter, and in and out
the barber's shop you will see and hear the most doing.
At the counter, from morning to night, one incessant
roll of clamour for beds and bills, and at the barber's
from dawn till dinner, a succession of unshorn Yankees
—a Yankee never shaves himself—submitting their
cheeks to the barber's razor, and their ears to his latest
news. You must not mind smoke, for you will be smothered with it; you must learn to tolerate chewing, or
you will get bilious; you must be indifferent to spitting,
or you will die of nausea. Montreal is crammed with
Americans; they are always here in great numbers,
and now the war has at least doubled them. South-
erners there are some, but Yankees preponderate; and
with all the occupants of the hotel, be they of what
nation they may, Yankee manners and customs are
certainly the fashionable thing. But you must take
no notice of these little eccentricities of our funny
cousins, and look at the master, the host himself. You

will see him smoking his cigar behind the counter,
and conversing with his visitors right and left, ex-
changing civilities with his new-comers, and shaking
hands with those who are leaving him—very attentive, very affable; in fact, exactly suited to his work,
and this is saying a great deal, for a formidable task
it must be to manage the details of the various departments in one of these gigantic establishments, and well
may the Yankees form their estimate of a man's smartness by his natural capacity for keeping an hotel.

Passing on through the hall, and ascending the
grand staircase, you will reach the reception-room—a
handsome *salon*, of large and lofty dimensions, with
anterooms and boudoirs attached to it; and here you
will find ladies and gentlemen in knots upon the chairs
and sofas, receiving visitors, or conversing amongst
themselves; and at the piano, in the centre of the
room, ten to one but you will see a precocious young
Yankee girl, of the age of sixteen perhaps, or under,
playing away before the assembled multitude, perfectly
regardless of the ears and eyes intent upon her—possibly even impudent enough to be practising her scales.
Further on you will come upon the dining-hall—an
elegant room like the last, entered by splendidly wide
passages or corridors, and filled with innumerable small
tables, which hold from four to eight or ten " covers"
each. The bedrooms are large, light, and airy, and
the ventilation of the building perfect.

3

It is a noisy life this, of course; but for a bachelor travelling "solo" I can imagine nothing more entertaining, and the living is cheap enough, when compared with the rates of our first-class hotels at home. Throughout this continent the charge is always so much per day, on the principle of the foreign "pensions," and at all the best hotels in Canada that charge is now two dollars, i. e., something over eight shillings. For this you get bed, breakfast, luncheon, dinner, tea, and supper—such a meal at each sitting as would feast a Londoner for a week—everything in fact but beverages other than water, or what an American elegantly terms "drinks." Breakfast goes on from 8 to 11, lunch from 1 to 2, dinner from 5 to 7, tea from 8 to 10, supper from 11 to 12, which signifies that to obtain any particular meal you must present yourself at some time between the two hours during which it is announced as obtainable.

Breakfast I think the most striking meal, and so I will ask you to accompany me to that. We will drop in, say at 9.30, sit down casually at any of the numerous tables which has a vacant place, and in a business-like tone of voice call for the carte. Now, having read Sala's letters we shall not be the least puzzled at the length of the list of viands and delicacies, nor shall we forget his celebrated account of his first breakfast on this continent, and the difficulty he had to get anybody to attend to him because he ordered only one dish. I must say that I did not quite believe the accuracy of that statement; but I find now that it is all absolutely true, and that a man, who sits down and orders an egg and a bit of toast, has just as much chance of getting any one to wait upon him, as he has of seeing the Thames pure, or the Conservatives in office, or any other physical impossibility.

So we are wise, and instead of selecting such dishes as we wish to try, point out to the waiter some two or three, of the fourteen, which we do not care to venture upon, and boldly order up the rest. The effect upon the waiter is magical; he puts us down as "smart ones," and civility and attention are at once secured. This was my plan on my first breakfast here, but the result of the order was somewhat alarming, for I found myself in about two minutes surrounded by a multitude of little oval dishes, on which were fish, steaks, chops, ham, chicken, turkey, rissoles, potatoes (boiled, roast and fried), cabbage, corn, cheese, onions and pickles, besides plates of hot rolls, buns, crumpets, toast and biscuits, flanked by a great jug full of milk and an enormous vessel of coffee. However, in the midst of my bewilderment, which seemed to puzzle the waiter, who had taken my order as a thing of every day occurrence, my friend the banker turned up, and with his help I succeeded in demolishing a considerable portion of the formidable array of dishes. But there was a Yankee next to us who ordered much the same as I had

thus unintentionally been burdened with, and what was
our astonishment to see him take *six* soft-boiled eggs, and
breaking them on the edge of a tumbler, drop in successively their respective yolks, and then, after two or
three whirls of his spoon in the glass, gobble them up
as an "appetiser," with a gurgle of delight that was
quite musical. This was only the preliminary canter.
You might have thought, perhaps, that at any rate he
was off on his raid upon the menu, but no, he was
only going through his paces previous to entering
upon the severer work before him, and when he *did* set
to, "my eye, warnt it a caution to snakes?" Fish,
steaks, chops, sausages, omelets, with vegetables of
several kinds, vanished like gnats before a thunder-
storm; coffee and tea chased one another down that
capacious throat, till, in less than three quarters of an
hour from the firing of the first shot, the table was
well nigh cleared, and a glass of iced milk brought to
a triumphant close this interesting performance.

Luncheon is served on the same liberal scale, dinner,
tea, and supper, ditto. It is no use trying to shirk a
dish, the waiters will insist on your trying everything,
so your only course is to try. Everybody tries every
dish; no one feels any compunction at leaving untouched what has been brought to him; waste is
immaterial, for meat is dirt-cheap, vegetables and fruit
abundant. All ages of either sex eat extravagantly;
no one looks astonished to see "a lovely plant of six-

teen summers," tucking down at breakfast kidneys, ham, and sausages after a tremendous plateful of fish ; no one stares to see a precocious youth of nine going straight through the dinner carte like a steam mowing-machine, puffing, and blowing, and spitting like an ill-used engine. It is a wonderful thing, truly, this Yankee appetite. I have been told in England that I myself am not deficient in this respect; I admit a considerable executive capacity—but set me down by a middle-aged Yankee lady, and by her side I am a mouse.

And yet with all this absorption of tissue-making material, there is, as Sala says, nothing to show for it —the men are all lanky, gaunt, fleshless, yellow-complexioned, haggard lamp posts; the women, lean, skinny, angular, all sharp corners and edges—waltzing with them, till you get used to it, must be torture. I do not know how to account for this invariable poverty of flesh—possibly it arises from over-feeding, as cats grow thin upon black beetles ; perhaps it is the physical result of an exaggerated sort of Banting's system ; and for my part I believe it almost impossible to get fat on meat three times a day—but I suppose the climate has much to do with it; Arctic frosts and tropical heats alternating in unbroken succession are not apparently adapted for the cultivation of anything like a corporation. North America may be the field of enterprise for every humbug under the sun, but Banting.

OTTAWA,

August 22nd.

I am now in the future capital of the two provinces
of Upper and Lower Canada. My journey here was
made by rail to Lachine, a few miles west of Montreal,
and thence by steamer up the Ottawa river. We had
anticipated a fine day's excursion, but unfortunately the
bush had taken fire, and the country for miles and
miles around was enveloped in clouds of smoke. At
times the fog was so thick that we had to stop and
drop our anchor; at others we were delayed by
frequent soundings; once we made a complete circuit,
and only discovered that we were returning to Montreal
when the sun broke through the fog upon the wrong side
of us. The Ottawa is a noble stream, called by the
Indians the "Grand River," varying from two miles
to one in breadth, and fringed by steep precipitous
banks, with pleasing landscape scenery above them.
But of this last I saw little or nothing, for the fog
scarcely cleared all day, and it was not till near
midnight that we reached the City of Ottawa. Since
my arrival here we have had some heavy rains, which
have extinguished the bush fire, that might, but for
this fortuitous downfall, have, I am told, burnt for
weeks. It is difficult to give you any idea of what one
of these fires is like. It is by no means easy to
convey an impression of what is signified by " the

bush." You must picture to yourself a tangled forest of closely-packed moderate-sized trees, with a dense undergrowth of shrubs; pines will be the most prevalent trees, but beech, maple, oak, sumac, walnut, and poplar, may all be included under the general term "pine forest." Imagine this mass of leaf to extend over a flat swampy area of hundreds of square miles, broken only here and there by the log hut of some lonely settler, or the freshly cleared corn-field of a newly arrived farmer. You must then suppose the underwood to have taken fire from some seemingly insignificant accident—a spark from a settler's pipe, perhaps, or a lighted ember from his log fire; and the heat of the sun's rays has so scorched the trees that they burn like touchwood down to the very roots, and so the fire is communicated to the parched turf or soil of the swamp, which smoulders away like peat for days and weeks and months, till rain falls and extinguishes the fire, after it has eaten its way into the earth perhaps three feet deep.

At present you would find it difficult to recognise in Ottawa the future metropolis of Canada. The inhabitants talk of it as Ottawa *City*, but it is much more like an overgrown village perched upon the top of a steep cliff, and straggles along the banks of the river and out away into the country beyond, as if all the houses were afraid of touching each other, and objected to the formality of a continuous street. No one seems

exactly to know why it has been selected as the seat of
Government.   Some tell me, to avoid throwing down
an apple of discord between the rival candidates,
Montreal, Quebec, and Toronto, by preferring any one
of them.   Some say it was selected by mistake; some,
I believe, think it was done by the Queen to spite the
Canadians.   But for whatever cause selected, it has
every element necessary for the creation of a great
city, and for the capital of the two provinces—a grand
river, a lovely site, a considerable distance between its
walls and the Yankee frontier, a very central position as
regards the Eastern and Western Provinces, and easy
access from all sides.   People are talking about the
proposed coalition of all the provinces now under British
rule, and saying that, if this federation scheme comes
off, Ottawa will never be permitted to retain her recently
acquired privilege; and that the seat of Government
must in that case remain, as it now is, in Quebec.   But
I cannot believe that any one who has ever seen the
new Parliament Buildings in course of erection at
Ottawa would be so barbarous as to demand the
destruction of that beautiful edifice.   The cost of the
new Houses has been enormous, and I do not think the
Canadians are likely to stand by and see this money
thrown to the winds.   If the Parliament Buildings are
not to be used, I cannot imagine a more flagrant
instance of reckless expenditure.

The Buildings consist of a central block, in which

are comprised the House or Chamber of the Legislative
Council (the Lords), and the House of Assembly (the
Commons), flanked by two wings, containing the
various Government offices, an arrangement which
brings them altogether under one roof; and fronted by
a spacious quadrangle, which will be ornamented with
trees. The back of the buildings runs parallel with the
river; and, as with our Houses at home, there is a
handsome terrace upon the river bank, only that the
bank is here 100 feet high, and the river is not a
sewer. The style is gothic, less ornamented than
St. Stephen's, and, I think, more substantial and
effective. It is the work of native talent, and the
Canadians may justly be proud, as they certainly are,
of this magnificent pile. Everything has been done in
the most costly style, and I think you would be as
much surprised as I was to come upon such a building
in what may be yet called the wilds of Canada.

The rain was coming down in tropical fashion when
we left the Houses of Parliament, but the Chaudière
Falls well repaid us the ducking we got in visiting
them. A fine bridge spans the river just below these
celebrated Falls, and from thence there is a view which
some people say is second only to Niagara in grandeur
and magnificence. There is a marvellous variety about
these Falls which I have never seen equalled elsewhere.
Arrayed in every imaginable form, in vast dark masses,
in graceful cascades, in tumbling spray, they present

the appearance of a hundred rivers struggling with the
rocks for a passage.   And when the hundred passages
are found, they plunge over the precipice into a deep,
dark basin, where they hiss, and boil, and seethe, and
whirl round in such hot haste as to verify the justice
of their name of *chaudière*, or caldron.   By the Falls
is one of the numerous saw-mills so prevalent in Canada, which we next visited, and well worth the visit
it was; but I have not time to tell you of the machinery, the noise, the saws, the bustle and business
of the establishment, for I must say a word about the
timber-slides, down one of which we took a ride, in
imitation, I suppose, of the Prince of Wales, who did
the same thing on his visit to Canada.

These slides are not uncommon in the Ottawa, being
an ingenious method of avoiding the cataracts, and
sending the timber from above to below the foaming
waters, without endangering the destruction of the raft
by collision with kindred rafts below, or annihilation
on the rocks.   They consist of a small miniature plan
of a series of canals and weirs, so managed that the
water never runs at so steep a gradient as to make it
break and foam, but passes smoothly over a succession
of inclined planes at an angle of forty-five degrees or
less.   At the bottom of each separate "shute" is a
wooden platform or "apron," upon which the rafters
are precipitated, and so preserved from diving down
under the surface by the impetus of their fall.   To

understand how the thing works, you must know that a
" raft" consists of thirty or forty separate " cribs," that
is, subdivisions or small rafts, each crib complete in
itself, and all bound together by cords and withes. In
coming down the rapids, or running the slides, the
raft is broken up into cribs, and so reduced to a more
manageable size ; and at the bottom of the slide, when
the descent of all is completed, the cribs are again
attached, and follow the current in one continuous raft
till more slides or rapids are reached, when the process
is repeated. They say that there is considerable danger
in shooting these slides, but it is much exaggerated.
Anyhow, I have done it once, and am safe. I do not
care to try it again ; but I wanted to be able to say
that I had done it, though, as Sidney Smith said, it
would have been just as easy to say that, without ever
doing it at all. My fellow-traveller and myself were,
however, *above* any such imposture, so we walked to
the head of the slide, got leave to go down with the
two steerers upon one, and, stepping on board, found
ourselves instantly in the current. It was a curious
sensation certainly, not over agreeable, but very exciting. In a few seconds we were upon the first inclined plane, and down we shot at a terrible pace, till,
in less time than I can tell it in, we lodged upon the
first "apron" with a bump and a crash that sent the
timbers jumping beneath our feet, and deluged the fore
part of the crib with spray and foam. Then on again,

before we had bare time to recover our balance, down the next incline, with another bump upon the next apron, and so on down two more, when we thought our troubles were at an end; but no, the crib in front of us had lost a spar in its downward passage, which had struck right athwart the current. There was no time to skedaddle, no chance of making a "strategic movement"; we hardly saw the obstacle in our way, when the end of our crib came upon it, and with a leap into the air, and a terrific splash on the descent into the water, we cleared the spar, and found ourselves in quiet water.

I am glad that I saw this little incident, for it gave me a good idea of the dangers with which the poor raftsmen have to contend. It is a hard life—harder than you or I, perhaps, could have imagined it possible for human beings to endure. Five hundred miles down the stream, through rapids and slides, had the brave *voyageurs* who manned our crib brought the timber island which was now their only home. Fourteen months' absence from civilised life amongst the bears and wolves of the backwoods had been necessary to fell, carry, and put together the hundreds of trees of which the whole raft was composed, and two months more would elapse before they would be safely moored at Quebec, beyond the dangers of the rapids and the slides. A little hut, no larger than a dog-kennel, with just a hole in front by which to creep in on hands and knees, was the only

covering from the rain and the storm ; a plank awning, on upright poles, formed their only apology for a
kitchen, and three or four tin pots and an iron caul-
dron composed the kitchen utensils, dinner-service, and
plate. But for all this indication of needy circumstances, there was an amount of pride amongst the
twenty or thirty occupants of the raft which, to a
stranger to the country, must be astonishing. Not
one of them would have received a sixpence for his
trouble in taking us down the slide ; each and all
would have treated the offer as an insult. And so it
is throughout Canada ; so it is, I hear, in the States.
No tipping waiters, no feeing porters ; their spirit of
independence forbids them to take any remuneration
from any one but their master. They hold themselves
in every bit as good a position as the visitor on whom
they wait ; *he* looks upon *them* as of equal station with
himself. No grades, no classes, no rank. We in
England are totally unable to realise this great levelling principle ; but it crops up in Canada as it does in
the States, at every turn you take. You will meet it
in the railway officials, who will quietly tell you to
carry your bag yourself; you will find it in the chambermaid, who will answer the bell or not, just as she
pleases, and if you politely suggest that you rang, will
coolly reply that she is " quite aware of it ;" you will
notice it everywhere in being addressed as " Mister"
—none but niggers will call you " Sir"—and find that

no request made of you is ever preceded by "if you please," no act of civility on your part followed by "thank you." Uniforms, liveries, and such-like frivolities of a bloated aristocracy, are alike discarded. The railway guard is dressed as yourself, the porters better; the captain and sailors of the steam-boats as town merchants and mechanics; the coachmen and grooms as private gentlemen. But with all this independence—this over-laboured acting out of the *liberté, égalité, fraternité* system—there are, as I see already, many redeeming points about it. There may be little courtesy in the manners of the people, but there is plenty of generosity; no French *politesse*, but a ready hand; no good breeding, but a willing heart. Society is in a rough, rude state out here, but there is something about it which I like, for all that; nothing like pride, nothing artificial, as amongst our upper classes at home, no gulf separating rich from poor; but I will not say more in this strain, or you will be looking on me as a Democrat, and I do not consider that I am so far gone as that at present.

The last few pages I have been writing at Toronto, where I arrived on the morning of the 25th; and here I am now, staying with my cousin and his wife at their cottage in Yorkville, a suburb of Toronto, about two miles from the central part of the city. I left Ottawa on the morning of the 23rd by the "cars"—you never go by train on this continent—to Prescott, on the

St. Lawrence about 120 miles above Montreal, where I took the steam-boat, for the purpose of running the rapids between Prescott and Montreal. The fall in the river between the two places is very great, so much so as to create a succession of rapids at various intervals, up which it is, of course, impossible for any boats to pass; but they venture to shoot them *down* the stream, performing the up journey through a long series of locks and canals. Having heard that it was a very exciting trip down the river, and a sight which I should regret to have missed, I determined to make the journey, though at the cost of retracing my steps towards the east; but I am satisfied that the trip well repaid me.

The scenery of the river here is not very striking, for the country is flat and uninteresting, so that I was glad to arrive at the first of the four Rapids which lay between us and Montreal. These were the Galop Rapids, the easiest of the four to run; in fact, there was little or no perceptible effect on the motion of the vessel, with the exception of an acceleration of an already high speed. But they only acted as a sort of *entrée* to the more piquant " sensation scenes" which met us further down. The Long Sault Rapids knocked us about much more, the current was fiercer, the interest of the surrounding country greater. There we went for two or more miles through the wild and roaring waters, while they dashed themselves in fury against the vessel, hissing and seething around as if panting to devour her. It was a grand sight to see how the flood heaves and bounds over the polished rocks, that vainly try to stem its course, and to ride over the lofty waves in which it rises in its wrath. It makes one's heart leap to think that one single slip on the pilot's part would hurl the ship to her grave; but the Indian to whose steady skill we trust, has been trained from boyhood to the work, and the four strong helmsmen at the wheel stand ready to obey the slightest signal. The steam is shut off, and the vessel dashes in amongst the rocks that glare through the water in terrible proximity, and down the narrow channel we are hurried with fearful rapidity on the crest of the rough, unruly waves, sometimes running straight upon a rock, as it would seem, but, by a well-timed turn of the wheel, shooting aside and past the danger in safety; sometimes bumping and rolling on the breakers as they buffet and beat upon our bows; and then on again down another incline, where the current glides unbroken through the shoals, till we are once more in the calm of the broad stream. The Cedar and Lachine rapids, equally exciting, and, perhaps, more dangerous, were safely passed in gallant style, and before dusk we were steaming under the giant arches of the tubular bridge up to the quay of Montreal.

Arriving there, I left again that night for Prescott by the Grand Trunk railroad. Slept at Prescott (a

miserable place), and on the 24th took the steamer to
Toronto. By noon our good ship was steaming into
the mazes of the Thousand Islands and their far-famed
lake—a labyrinth of loveliness which no water scenery
that I know equals. It smacks rather of an Irish
"bull" to say it, but there are some eighteen hundred
of these islands scattered about in careless irregularity
in the current of the river; some small, so small that
they seem only a few yards in circumference; others,
again, some miles in circuit, all rich in verdure and
fringed with trees down to the very margin of the lake.
Ever and anon we hurry through a narrow channel
between two islets, that almost jam us in their grasp,
apparently rushing into a *cul-de-sac* from which no
exit is visible; but as we near the seemingly impenetrable barrier of rock, an opening discloses itself
through which we turn only to find ourselves similarly
land-locked again. And so it is for nearly fifty miles,
the same land-locking, the same mode of egress, while
we sail along in the midst of a continuation of rock
and tree, browns and greens of every hue, such as I
think the Scotch Highlands cannot surpass in depth
and variety.

After leaving Kingston we were soon out of sight
of land—a novel idea in the case of fresh-water,—
and we had a roughish night, too, upon the lake;
but the morning was bright and clear, and by eight
o'clock we were at the wharf of Toronto.

4

Toronto is a very pleasant town. I am not sure that I do not prefer it to Montreal. The streets are wide, the houses good, and the suburbs and parks beautiful. Then there are some fine buildings to be seen : the English and French Cathedrals ; the University, in the style of the new Parliament Houses of Ottawa ; and the famous Osgoode Hall, which has been talked of as a model for our new law-courts in Lincoln's Inn, and which may well be followed, for I do not see how it is possible to have any handsomer, better arranged building. I certainly was most surprised to find a young colony like this in the possession of such an institution. The courts are perfect ; large, lofty, and well ventilated ; fitted with comfortable seats for the bar, convenient means of access to them, and luxurious cushions for the Q.Cs., which are, I should fear, pre-eminently conducive to sleep. But, for all that, I do not see why it is necessary to keep the English Bar awake by putting them on seats upon which it is almost impossible to be decently comfortable. There is a handsome library, too, which is at present chiefly shelves, but I suppose the books will arrive in time ; if not, they can easily send to Chancery Lane for a few boxes of those old editions of legal textbooks, which are said to be seen now and then packing for the colonies. The Judges and the Bar are very much what they are at home, except that they go bare-headed and eschew wigs ; a practice that entails an amount of hair-brushing to which the hard-worked professional adviser cannot be expected to sacrifice his client's interest. A wig covers a multitude of short-comings.

I have done little since I have been in Toronto but walk about the town, ride in the street-cars, eat, drink, and enjoy myself; and to-morrow I am off with my cousin on a tour to the West and the Mississippi. This is a grand time for travelling in the States, for the railway fare is at ordinary times exceedingly low, and, being fixed by statute, has not been affected by the present exceptional rise in prices. Consequently, to those who have the luck to bear in their pockets English gold or its equivalent, the expense of a journey is a mere song. Gold, when I landed, stood at the extraordinary height of 260. A timely whisper hinted to me a coming fall, so with more curiosity than confidence in the solvency of the United States, I invested largely in greenbacks. Ten minutes after my purchase the next telegram sent it down 10 per cent. I begin to feel stealing over me the contagious influence of the gambling fever, with which the whole continent is infected, from Wall Street even to Toronto. Fancy my excitement if the next telegram sends it down another ten points, and then another, and another ten! And how if it rushes up? I dare not think of the alternative, nor have I time, for I am off at once to Niagara, where a treat is in store for me on which I have long been reckoning.

III.

NIAGARA TO BUFFALO.

Chicago,
September 4th, 1864.

I am now fairly amongst the Americans, imbibing all I can of the manners and customs of " the Great West," and attempting to get an insight into the character of the people ; but they are at present a tremendous puzzle to me, unlike any nation whose representatives I have ever met with ; as little like plain, honest, steady-going Englishmen, as I believe it possible for a people professing to speak the English language to be. In fact I find that before I came out here I knew as little about them as I do of the inhabitants of the unexplored wilds of Central Africa, indeed, I might almost say less, for I dare say it would not be difficult to guess with tolerable precision at the probable characteristics of those savage races ; but I do not believe the *clairvoyance* of Dr. Cumming himself could have prophesied to me the strange features of this unique country and its people. But of this more anon. My last letter, I think, brought me up to Toronto, where I spent four pleasant days with my cousin and his wife, in their comfortable cottage, and told you what I had seen in their pretty little city; so that I will now conduct you across the lake of Ontario to the world's wonder—Niagara.

We started for the Falls by steamer on the morning of Tuesday, August the 30th, landing on the American side by the mouth of the Niagara River, and proceeding by rail to the largest of the several hotels on that side, "The Cataract." The journey was only a short one, noticeable for nothing beyond the curious feature presented by the confluence of the Niagara River and the broad waters of the Lake; where, as with the Rhone and the Arve at Geneva, the Ottawa and the St. Lawrence at Montreal, the Gulf Stream and the Atlantic Ocean, there seems to be such a want of chemical affinity between the two currents that their waters will not intermingle; for miles you could trace the line of contact, so distinctly marked that you might fancy some hidden breakwater kept the two apart. Our steamer took us about eight miles up the Niagara River, a very pretty sail through lofty wooded cliffs, and thence "the cars" whisked us along the top of the American shore, skirting the edge of the precipice at such a giddy height as made me shudder to look down and see the angry rapids foaming and fretting beneath us. Half an hour, and we were in sight of the cloud of mist that day and night rises

from the Falls, high above the forest and the town;
and another half-hour, and, after a very distant peep at
the Falls themselves, we were landing from the cars
within a few yards of the great Cataract Hotel.

The house stands close upon the edge of the upper
rapids of the river, just where they race and hustle
through the rocks, as they prepare themselves for their
final leap into the abyss beyond. There is no view
from the windows of the actual Falls, but the scenery
around is beautiful. The rooms open out upon the
rapids, the drawing-room, a splendid apartment, with a
balcony running round it, from which we took our first
view of the magnificent scene; our second look at the
same grand picture being obtained from a wooden pier
thrown out upon some boulder-stones that have lodged
in the midst of the current. Opposite to the Hotel
lies Goat Island, concealing from the eye the Canadian
Falls, but adding to the beauty of the rapids by its
own exquisite loveliness of foliage. It is this island
that divides the waters of the river into two currents
that are precipitated over the Canadian and American
Falls. The Canadian or Horse-shoe Fall, is far the
grander of the two. The American, of less volume,
is at right angles with the former, some little distance
lower down the river, for the Canadian Fall, the more
powerful, has eaten away the upper bed of the stream
faster than her sister Fall, and so retreated, as it were,
several hundred yards higher up the gorge.

Passing by a suspension bridge which connects. Goat Island with the mainland, we walked to the lowest corner of the islet, and stood at once upon the brink of the precipice down which thunders the American Fall. No scene that I have ever witnessed overwhelmed me with such uncontrollable wonder as that which I looked upon, when I first stood on the margin of the plunge of the mighty cataract. The height, the power, and volume of the Falls exceeded my utmost expectations. I had been told that I should be disappointed; but if there be any who have been, I cannot conceive what their imagination could have anticipated. I own I expected more noise, but the state of the atmosphere affects that, and the roar of the Falls, like that of Bottom and Earl Russell, will at one time be as paltry and insignificant as at another it will be grand and terrifying. I should like to have the power to give you some idea of the sublimity of the scene, but it is utterly useless to attempt a description of what is wholly indescribable. The tortuous surgings of the rapids, the sudden calmness at the brow of the cataract, the majestic sea-green curve in which the liquid mass glides over the edge of the precipice, the silvery ringlets into which it is broken up soon after leaving the brink of the rock, the feathery mist in which it showers down into the cloud of spray that ever veils the last fifty feet of the Fall, and the infernal writhe and whiteness in which it reappears in the depths of the abyss,—all these wondrous features of the Queen of Cataracts must be seen, watched, sat beside for hours and days, before the mind can grasp the magnificence of the scene. But we were as yet only in sight of the American Fall. A walk along the further side of Goat Island brought us in view of the Canadian Fall, and then I found that I had been expending my fullest admiration and astonishment upon a mere thread of Niagara, the thousandth part of its volume and grandeur, for there was before me again the same glorious scene that I have so briefly sketched ; only it was a thousand times intensified.

We ascended, and took a view from every one of the numerous points from which tourists are expected to survey the Falls, and paid all those preposterous sums which tourists are invariably doomed to give—for Niagara has its excursionists by thousands, and its " look-outs," " summer-houses," " retreats," " staircases," " perilous seats," and such-like attractions for an excursion party; but it is less cockneyfied, for all that, than many a place that I have visited—less so than Chamouni and the Rigi, and such favorite resorts that do not draw half so many visitors as the Falls. Having done our duty as pure excursionists, and been bled accordingly, we took a carriage and drove off to the Canadian side of the river, crossing by the famous suspension bridge which connects the British and American territories. It is an extraordinary triumph of engineering skill to have thrown across the yawning gulf such a mass of weighty metal as here spans the torrent. How it ever got there, is to my mind a dark inexplicable mystery, the solution of which I am not mathematician or engineer enough to see; but there it is, to testify, in conjunction with the tubular bridge of Montreal and the canals of the St. Lawrence, to the ingenuity and enterprise of the people of Canada.

The bridge is two miles below the falls, so that the view thence is too distant to be effective; but the drive up to them along the Canadian cliff, past "The Clifton House," the great Canadian hotel, is, I think, the most beautiful road I have ever seen. It is from this side that you get, in one grand comprehensive landscape, the whole length of the American and Canadian Falls, with the steep precipices of Goat Island between them, and the cliffs of the American bank further down the gorge, and above them the roofs, and spires, and gables of the town peering out from amid the forest that forms the background of the picture. Table Rock is a lofty shelving promontory of limestone jutting out from the Canadian shore close upon the brink of the plunge of the great Horse-shoe Fall; and there we sat, as all tourists do, and gazed in rapture at the marvels of nature unfolded around, above, beneath us. I cannot tell you what we saw; you could not depicture it to yourself if I could. I will only say that that one view from Table Rock would

repay any one a journey from the farthest corner of
the world.   All the landscapes I have ever seen—all
the snow-pictures of the Alps—all the coast-scenery of
the Mediterranean—all the lochs and moors of the
Scotch Highlands—sink into insignificance when compared with the incomparable grandeur of Niagara. It
is not the Falls themselves alone that create the magnificence of the scene ; but the beauty of the landscape,
of which they are the centre, adds a hundredfold to
their intrinsic splendour.   The setting is worthy of
the gem. But it is useless to tell you how I sat and
wondered at the majesty of the view from Table Rock ;
you must go and stand there yourself, and then you
will be amazed, as I was, at the all-absorbing interest
of the scene, and ponder, as I did, upon the marvellous
force and volume of the waters that every second
plunge down the heights before you, and wonder whence
comes the inexhaustible supply, and whither it goes,
and how many a long roll of countless summers has
looked on the same unvaried scene ; and then you will
wish, perhaps, to put down on paper some little me-
mento of what you saw and felt, and find, I dare say,
as I do, that the attempt is futile.

But a distant view of the Falls gives but a faint idea
of their solemn grandeur.   To comprehend them in
their awe-inspiring sublimity, you must descend to the
base of the cliff, and walk in amongst the spray, and
under the curve of their flight down the precipice, and

see the terrific power of their waters and the impotence
of man beside them; in fact, you must do as I did,
make the expedition to the " Cave of the Winds," and
then you will have impressed upon your mind, perhaps
too forcibly, the detail of the more awful properties of
Niagara, which a close acquaintance can alone reveal
to you.

The " Cave" lies underneath the American Fall; the
trip is decidedly a perilous one, but it is "*the* thing,"
and so, to be fashionable, I did it. The party of ad-
venturers consisted of eight, with a guide, a French
Canadian. At a house by the foot of the Fall,. we
were provided with a dress, or at least an apology for a
costume, the very queerest, oddest-looking, scantiest set
of garments in which I have ever appeared in public.
The suit consisted of a remarkably thin threadbare
flannel shirt, a much thinner and much more threadbare pair of flannel drawers, a pair of flannel socks or
slippers, and a cord round the waist; the whole sur-
mounted by an oilskin skull-cap. I never felt more
like the maniac who persisted in confining his
street toilette to "hatband and straps," or realised
more painfully the confusing effect of the penetrating
glances of half a dozen young ladies, than on the
occasion when our little party in Indian file threaded
the gauntlet of the inquisitive ones who had drawn up
to see us enter the cave. But a bold face and buoyant
spirits were necessary for the work that lay before us.

After a few words of counsel from the guide about not being frightened, but keeping straight ahead, and energetic assurances that we should *not* be drowned—though we should be sure to fancy that would be the result, for every one, he said, thought so at first—we descended some steps that led right down into the spray of the Fall, and at the bottom came upon a path or narrow ledge that wound along the cliff inside the archway of the Fall.

From the moment that we left the stairs, we got into a fine pelting rain that gradually increased in weight and volume, till it bore down upon our skull-caps like hail upon a skylight. But the cave lay on the further side of the sheet of water, through which we had to get as best we could. How that was, I cannot tell you. The guide led the way into the steam and turmoil, bending himself nearly double to keep the beating spray from his nostrils, and clinging on to the slimy rock, for the foothold was slippery and difficult. I believe I did the same, but I cannot say. The guide was immediately lost to our view; and all that I could hear, amid the thunder of the cataract beside us, was an injunction to push on when it came to the worst, for the illogical reason that it was shorter to get beyond the sheet of water than to turn back. I cannot describe to you what a terrifying scene it was—how the waters roared around us—how the stifling spray beat upon our faces, so as to drive all the breath out of our bodies—how the wind, caused by the falling mass of water, blew about in a thousand blinding gusts (as if old Æolus had untied every single sack, and let out the whole of his seminary for a general holiday), dashing the rain into our faces and chests, or driving it against our backs and legs, or both ways at once with equal fury—or what I did, or what I saw. I do not know where, or why, or how I went. I only know that I went down into this watery hell, and came up again uninjured, but very much out of breath and awfully frightened, half blinded, more than half deafened, and three-quarters drowned. The rest was comparatively simple—merely a scramble through the mist over slimy polished rocks, a swim across a little pool, and a climb to a chair fixed on a rugged crag, when I found myself out in front of the Fall, with a splendid view of it looking upwards before me, and, the greatest novelty of all, a circular rainbow all around me, at times too even doubled. Five minutes' rest upon the crag, and we retraced our steps—for there was no other way back again to terra firma—and then in again amongst the rain and the din of waters, more panting for breath, more struggling with the wanton gusts, more bewildering of the eye and ear, more clinging for bare life to the slimy rock, and climbing up the slippery staircase; and so we reached the more hospitable regions of the open air, and again ran the gauntlet of the curious eyes that awaited our return to daylight—less nervous, perhaps, about their gaze, after what we had faced below, but very much more *dégagés* and disreputable.   I do not know that I should care to make the expedition again, though I met one rather stout Canadian, who told me he went down regularly twice a week, under the idea that it would reduce his fat; but I am not by nature amphibious, and I consider the feat well worthy of the certificate with which the guide presents the visitors before they leave, testifying to the fact that they have " passed through the Cave of the Winds."

The Cataract Hotel was filled with guests—all the Hotels always are—and there was an amount of style about them which was very different from anything I had seen in Canada.   Dinner was served with profuse liberality— dinner toilettes as profuse in their extravagance, colour everywhere, gaiety ditto ; a whirl of excitement, dress, flirtation, and fun; and all for $4 a day, which at the rate at which I sold my gold, was equal to 6s. 9d. sterling, including music in the evening by a first-rate band, and such a Charlotte Russe as I never tasted elsewhere, and ice-creams, and lots of back hair, and no crinoline, and *such* blue eyes, and endless other luxuries, that made me very loth to leave the Falls, as we at length did, *en route* for the Great West.

Our first station was Buffalo.   An hour's ride in the cars brought us to the depot or terminus, here pronounced " deapo," and five minutes more to the

American House, the chief hotel of that city. Buffalo is a handsome city of 100,000 inhabitants, just at the lower end of Lake Erie. The main street is one of the finest streets I know—a broad, well-paved avenue stretching from the quays on the lake shore for a distance of three miles back into the country; the lower end composed of enormous warehouses, stores, shops, and hotels—the upper portion of splendid private residences. We could not help noticing how different from Canada was the aspect of everything we saw in this the first great American city which lay in our road; how busy were the wharves and the streets leading to them, how fine were all the buildings, how tasty and elegant the "boulevards" running into the main street from the various suburbs of the city; how wealthy and prosperous everything looked and everybody; how "go-ahead" was legibly written on all that met our eyes, and echoed in every word that struck our ears. There is a peculiar characteristic about these new American cities which is unlike anythink I have ever seen upon our side of the Atlantic. The people themselves express this trait by the word "fast," an epithet in which they take the greatest delight, for they are everlastingly assuring you that this much-prized feature is to be found in their national character to an extent unknown in the Old World. "We are a very fast people, yess----sirrrr----eeeeee." And true enough there is a rapidity of development in their national and individual life, in their ideas and institutions, which in great measure justifies their vainglory; the egg is prematurely hatched, the fœtus artificially developed, and yet the pace does not kill. The wheels run easily, the machinery is well oiled; there is less hitch or clog about it than in Canada. In Buffalo, and in Cleveland, which I passed through yesterday, and still more in Chicago, where I now am, there is a smartness, a brilliancy, a dash about everything, the like of which I did not see in the Canadian cities, still less have I seen it in steady-going old England. I do not know how to explain to you what I mean—I hardly know how to realize to myself what it is that makes this people differ so from any other with whom I have come in contact; but there certainly is amongst these Western men a marked element of dissimilarity from all European races, a peculiarity of character which I have never seen sufficiently brought out in the writings of any newspaper correspondent or author. In fact, the more I see of the Americans, the more plainly I see how great and lamentable an ignorance of each other the people of two continents may live in, in spite of all the modern facilities of communication, when they have 3,000 miles' breadth of water interposed between them, and no direct reason for improving their acquaintance.

Soon after our arrival the intelligence reached the town that General M'Clellan had been nominated at

the Chicago Convention. I was disappointed at having
missed the opportunity of seeing and hearing the
orators of the day, but I could not manage otherwise;
so I had to content myself with hearing the matter
discussed in Buffalo, where the news of the General's
nomination was enthusiastically received. Bonfires
were lit, and guns fired, and flags waved, and windows
broken, till a very late hour of the night; for "little
Mac," as he is familiarly called by his friends, is high
in favour just now at Buffalo; not that he is considered the best representative of his party, but the
Democratic "platform," which he is intended to
typify, is the popular one in the great trading
cities of the West, where, as far as I can see, the
Republican "ticket" will curry no favour. To those
who are accustomed to look upon Conservatism as the
religion of the rural districts, and Liberalism as the
faith of the towns, it must seem strange to find the
order of things exactly reversed on this continent; for
the country farmers are here the Radicals, and the
Conservative element is affected in the populous cities.

This is, of course, a very interesting time to travel
here, with the approaching election so near at hand,
but it is extremely difficult to get with anything like
certainty at the probable result of the coming contest.
Both parties are now equally confident of success, and
I have, as yet, little means of judging which is the
stronger. Besides, people are very cautious about

5

what they say on the subject of politics; they will
venture readily enough upon general remarks, but beyond these they are unwilling to trust themselves.
Indeed, I have only met with one man who opened
his heart to me, and gave me what I suppose to have
been his real ideas; but he may have been a spy only
sounding me. Still there is plenty of talk and squab-
ble amongst themselves, for party feeling, running at
all times far higher than it does with our less excitable
politicians, is naturally swollen by the flood of. war;
and Democrats and Republicans have a gulf between
them which no coalition could bridge over.

Two of my fellow-voyagers from England joined my
cousin and myself at Buffalo, and the following
evening our party of four left by one of the Lake
Erie steamers for Cleveland, on the Southern shore,
intending to take the cars thence to Chicago, a distance in all of 530 miles. But that is a mere nothing
to the erratic people of this continent—a distance
which I believe they would travel, if they could, every
day of the year. For travelling is cheap, and, though
not rapid (in the West), extremely comfortable.

In the first place the water-communication is on
such a scale as no other quarter of the world can equal,
and the steamers that make use of it are in every way
excellent. Then the open cars are well adapted for a
land where all stand upon the same level, and though
the track is not well laid, slow travelling obviates

jolting; and, in a country like this, where food is cheap and labour dear, and time proportionately of little value, speed is an object of less moment than in England, where every minute has its specific value in gold, and necessity drives men to a deadly struggle with time in which they strive to crowd sixty such minutes into every second. But here life is not such a burden; money is made with half the labour, and goes more than twice as far; food is cheap, land the same, house-rent not yet high, labour extremely scarce, and wages good enough, I should have thought, to populate the country ten times as fast as the present immigration does. A dollar a day (gold) and *board besides* is the princely salary of the commonest labourer: my wonder is that one single Irishman remains at home. Mechanics, clerks, cashiers, are paid almost fabulous wages: I cannot imagine how such high prices can be afforded by the masters, but there is little or no saving of money; it comes with marvellous ease and rapidity, and goes as rapidly again. There is no slaving to lay by for the future; none of the bee's instinctive providence for the frosts, none of the beaver's care for her young. Why should there be? A man gives his children a decent education, and considers that his duty is done. What reason has he for doing more? He has risen from the lowest ranks himself, his son can make his way as well; if not, he may go to his Satanic majesty's dominions. And so

he does in three cases out of five. Aristocracy is a
thing so odious in the eyes of the people, old family
pride and what they call "English feudalism" are so
nauseous in this land of freedom, that a man who
starts without a penny in the world has a better chance
often of success than the millionaire's son with his
pockets full.   Then life is short, good old age, so
common at home, is here very rarely met with, so
saving of money for selfish reasons is a thing worse than
useless : a butterfly's life, a short and a merry one, is
to be said, I suppose, of no people with such truth as
of the Americans.

Well then, if money is made so fast, and is so little
worth keeping, it must be spent, and how can it be
done more agreeably to the restless character of the
makers of it, than by travelling ?   Locomotion is
made very easy ; the arrangements are perfect ; everybody plays into everybody's hands ; the hotels, the
trains, the boats, and the omnibuses all work together
most harmoniously.   If the train by which you are to
travel stops anywhere to enable the passengers to dine,
you will not get dinner at the hotel ; if the boat gives
a breakfast, you must take it on board, or go without ;
if the train gets in by supper time, you are expected
to look for nothing to eat at the refreshment rooms,
but wait till you reach your hotel.   Then the steam-
boats all "connect" with the trains, and the trains
with the steamboats, and the omnibuses with both.

Where the cars run in connection with the boats, the line is carried right down to the side of the wharf; where no water communication exists, the railway runs down the principal street, and the depot is in the centre of the town; for an American does not look upon a railroad as a nuisance to be kept out of sight down amongst the back slums of a city, but treats it as what it really is, the greatest comfort and convenience of the present century. Add to all this the low rate of the fares, fixed in most cases by Act of Congress, and thereby prevented from participating in the general rise of prices. For me, with the advantage of the favorable exchange, the fares are ridiculous. It cost me barely more than a guinea to travel from Buffalo to Chicago, 530 miles, and this included a bed, supper and breakfast, on board the steamboat to Cleveland. It is a marvel to me that John Bull and all the nations of Europe, whose gold is abundant, do not come out and travel here. The fare I have mentioned is not unusually low; indeed I have seen advertisements of some fares that would sound to your ears much more absurd; and yet you must remember that excursion trains are here unknown; these are the ordinary fares, which remain unaltered all the year round.

Having, then, every inducement to travel, the Americans turn out in extraordinary numbers; every one does his or her proper number of miles in thousands

every year.   Country seats are unknown, and some
change being necessary to keep them alive, the people
rush to and fro in a restless way that would surprise
you, were you to see it.   One old gentleman told me
that he took his family to the seaside, 1800 miles,
every year, and 1800 back, with less trouble and concern, I dare say, than a Londoner would make about
going down to Ipswich.   A youth of fifteen thinks
himself ill-used, if he has not seen all the great cities
of his country and the interior of every State; a girl
of thirteen considers her education neglected if her
parents have not allowed her to see more.   But it is
not only in summer that the traffic is so enormous;
it is all the year round just the same.   People in the
East are sure to have friends and relations in the
West, who have come to grief and migrated thither,
and the truants must be visited every year.   Adven-
turers and prodigals from the West must be welcomed
as often in their deserted homes.   So the nation is in
a chronic state of "fidgets."   Men and women of
every age, babies in arms, and men who are called old,
females almost as numerous as the males, crowd the
cars, stuff the steamboats, overwhelm the omnibuses,
and storm the hotels.

This fearful overcrowding of all the conveyances is
the only nuisance which I have hitherto experienced in
travelling, and in the cars it has sometimes amounted
to something more than a personal inconvenience.

You have heard, of course, of the extravagant respect paid by the people of the West to what I cannot conscientiously call here the softer sex—their frames are much too angular and uninviting. Now, I do not believe in all this exaggerated deference to the weaker sex. If I have paid my fare for a seat in the cars, I do not see why I should give it up to any ill-clad woman who enters after me. If I have taken the trouble to secure a berth in the steamboat, I do not know on what principle of equity I am called upon to give it up to the ugliest woman who may ask for it. In the street cars the evil is far worse. No matter how full of hard-worked men the car may be, any fish-woman with her basket on her arm will hail it, knowing that some gentleman must rise for her. It is an unnatural, untrue, mock respect, productive of ill consequences in the female mind, and, besides, totally superficial; for with all this unhealthy outward show of deference, there is not half that quiet easy courtesy and simple unaffected homage which are the acknowledged tribute to the fair sex amongst the educated classes of England.

I am getting behind-hand, I am afraid, in my account of what I have seen and done, for I have been two days in Chicago, and have not yet carried you more than half way here. But the novelty of everything and everybody gives me so much to say, that I must plead this as my excuse for taking you over the ground at first so slowly. You will overtake me, 1 have no doubt, when my supply of first impressions is all let off.

IV.

CLEVELAND TO CHICAGO.

St. Paul's,
September 10th.

I have a good deal of work before me, so I must return at once to my story, and tell you that, after a good night's rest on board the steamboat, we found ourselves in the morning off Cleveland harbour; and, landing, proceeded to look at the city. It is a very pretty place, much like Buffalo, though of smaller dimensions; but more tastefully laid out, especially in the suburbs, where the merchants' houses are really beautiful. Certainly these Americans have wonderful taste. I thought that they were such utilitarians that architecture, decoration, and ornament would have been in their eyes foolishness and insanity. But I never was more mistaken. Utilitarians as they are, above every other nation of the earth, they are naturally great lovers of ornament, and in their private residences they display an amount of taste and knowledge of "the beautiful," which the Italian villas can hardly exceed. With the Americans, as with the people of Italy, there seems to be a peculiar appreciation of decorative art. Like the Italian, the American seems to demand art, not as a luxury, but as a necessity. If he cannot have it in good material he will have it in bad; but in some shape or other he will gratify his eye, without which his vision would be blindness. If his means be ample, he will have his house of stone or marble; if he cannot have it in stone, he will have it in stucco or painted iron; if he cannot afford that, he will cover his house with creepers, or plant beside it some elegant tree; but satisfy his craving he certainly will. Trees are a great feature in every town and city. The first thing which an American does, in laying out a new street, is to plant on either side some ornamental timber; so that every city becomes a map of Parisian "boulevards," which add warmth and colour to the buildings, and in the summer heats are incalculably useful.

There is no particular object of interest in Cleveland, as indeed there can hardly be in any city in so new a country as this; there is of course an excellent hotel of unwieldy size and tremendous business, and if it does not always live in my memory for the almost inconceivable nastiness of its marble floors, notwithstanding the gigantic proportions of its spittoons, it certainly will for a dinner which I there had for the sum of 1s. 8¼d. sterling, such as I could not have had in London or Paris for twenty times that sum. I have diligently preserved the bill of fare for your special edification. I wish some of our English Hotel-Jews could see it and note the charge. (See next page.)

Dinner over, we proceeded to the station, and engaged berths in the sleeping car for Chicago. This was my first introduction to this great institution of the model Republic, and for the life of me I cannot see why our night journeys in England should not be performed in some such comfortable way. You know, I dare say, what these cars are like, for you will recollect that there was one to be seen at the last exhibition, of 1862. I know no reason why a similar system should not be adopted at home; though I do not suppose our English ladies would take to them very readily; at any rate I am sure they would never turn in, as they do here, in the same car with the men, quite promiscuously.

But a woman can do, and does, here, many things that she could never do in England; one of which, that speaks more for the American people than any other fact I know, is, that she can travel unattended from one end of the Union to the other in absolute security from insult or interference of officious gallantry. The sleeping car, being a novelty, was very amusing, and our novitiate equally amusing to the old travellers, who were continually bothering us with questions about our system, and Mr. Briggs's murder.

DINNER.

CLEVELAND, O., SEPT. 2, 1864.

SOUP.
Tomato with Rice.

FISH.
Trout, Baked, Claret Sauce.

BOILED.
Leg of Mutton, Caper sauce.
Smoked Bacon with Greens.
Corned Beef with Turnips.
Smoked Beef Tongue, with Spinach.
Beef, à la mode.
Ham with Cabbage.

ROAST.
Ribs of Beef, with Horseradish.
Lamb, Mint sauce.
Ham, Champagne sauce.
Pork, Apple sauce.
Loin of Veal.
Saddle of Mutton with Jelly.

ENTREES.
Lamb Chops, Saute à la Jardinaire.
Calf's Brains, au Grattin, Sauce Alemaud.
Veal Chops, brended, à la Italian.
Kidneys, saute, Champagne sauce.
Friccasee of Young Chickens.

Maccaroni baked with Cheese.
Pancakes, with Jelly, à la Celestine.
Fillets of Trout, Tomato sauce.
Breast of Lamb, stuffed, au fine Herbs.
Chicken Giblets, stewed, Wine sauce.

COLD DISHES.
Spiced Beef, à la mode.
Beef Tongue.
Leg of Mutton.

Pressed Corn Beef.
Loin of Veal.
Round of Beef.

VEGETABLES.
Boiled Potatoes.
Mashed Potatoes.
Baked Potatoes.
Hominy.
Green Corn.

Egg Plant.
Turnips.
Beets.
Onions.
Sucotash.

Squashes.
Cabbage.
Snap Beans.
Rice and Milk.
Tomatoes.

RELISHES.
Cold Slaw.
Cucumbers.
Mixed Pickles.

Lettuce.
French Mustard.
Worcester Sauce.

Horse Radish.
Old Cheese.
Pepper Sauce.

PASTRY AND DESSERT.
Rice Pudding.   Apple Pie.   Custard Pie.   Peach Puffs.   Jelly Tartlets.
Sponge Cake.   Fruit Cake.   Ice Cream.

FRUIT.
Melons.   Raisins.   Apples.   Pears.   Nuts.   Peaches.

FRENCH COFFEE.

Indeed I have hardly met an American who has not
at one time or another, in the course of conversation,
inquired of me whether such an assault is not of frequent occurrence. The papers have made more fuss
about it than our English journals ever did. They
look upon the system as an evidence of the tyrannical
oppression to which a people will submit in the hands
of a bloated aristocracy, and tell you, with virtuous indignation, that no American citizen would ever allow
himself to be locked up like a common vagabond. The
newspapers teem with puritanical bosh about " the
profligacy of the English railway cars," " sin on
wheels," and such like sensational headings. Why the
nation has gone mad upon the incident of this unfortunate murder—the solitary instance, so far as I
know—is more than I can conceive ; but, excepting the
great fight between Sayers and Heenan, I do not suppose any subject of English history has more interested the American nation than this mysterious exploit
of Mr. Müller.

I had a comfortable night's rest ; comfortable, I
mean, considering the time and place of my courtship
of Morpheus ; but they do not lay the track here with
half the care with which our engineers put it down at
home ; indeed the distances to be covered are so enormous, that in the present state of the country it could
not pay to execute the lines with the same finish. So
the rails are laid with little or no precision, upon logs of

wood, which are called "ties," tossed down promiscuously upon the road, which is not half levelled. Nothing in particular keeps the "ties" in their places, for they are covered with no ballast, not even sunk an inch into the ground. Less can be seen to preserve the rails on the "ties"; and on the older portions of the Grand Trunk of Canada, the worst specimens of railway engineering I have ever ridden over, the rails lie as if they partook of the general independence of the country, each bar of iron a separate entity, quite distinct from and unconnected with its neighbouring bar, with inches often of vertical and lateral deviation between the two; which irregularity makes itself painfully evident to any one that has unluckily taken a seat over a wheel, by a series of bumps and jars, and shocks to the nervous system that are simply excruciating. But the Grand Trunk is improving; probably the complaints of the public induced the manager, a Canadian notoriety, to take a seat for five minutes over a wheel. He is a fat podgy personage, and it would tell on him fearfully—but, however that may be, the lines are being re-laid, and the people are no longer to be subjected to a corporal punishment to which English school discipline is a joke.

After a dabble in a teaspoonful of water, and a scrape with a bit of an old sack, in a box, which is dignified with the title of " wash room"—for the American cars are, as it were, moveable hotels, with every accommodation complete (including what, I think, from a sanitary point of view, had very much better not be there), I took a walk up and down the train, with the rest of my fellow-passengers, and thereby improved my appetite for the breakfast which we were to take at a station on the road. It was very well served, for the Americans understand this sort of thing quite as well as our French neighbours; and by the time I had smoked a cigar, and taken another walk, to digest my meal, the cars reached Chicago.

I now proceed to give you some account of this city, and first of the hotel at which I have been staying.

The Tremont House is the largest hotel that I have seen as yet, though I am told that it is beaten by those in New York. It is a splendid block of buildings, arranged very much upon the principle of the St. Lawrence Hall at Montreal, with the exception that the basement floor of the block is occupied by shops in the exterior, while the inner portion is devoted to the offices and kitchens. The reception rooms are gigantic, the dining rooms still more so, and the noise and bustle of the establishment surpass anything you can imagine. It would be all very comfortable if it were not for that notorious American peculiarity, tobacco-chewing, and its unavoidable consequences.

I am sorry to have to trouble you with so unpleasant a subject, but the fact is that, if I am to touch upon the national characteristics of the people, I do not see how I can omit one which is undoubtedly, to a stranger, the most noticeable of all. It is a matter which every visitor to this country has written and talked of, and I had heard on all sides so much about it, that I thought the evil much exaggerated. But now that I have come and seen for myself the extravagant extent to which this beastly practice is carried, and the disgusting filthiness of habits attendant upon it, I can assure you that Russell and Sala have not said a word too harsh on this subject, which is a crying stain upon the enlightened civilisation of the people. I know I am in the West only as yet, where refinement of manners is little cultivated at present, and I am assured that tobacco-chewing, though by no means uncommon in the East, is there conducted in a much more gentlemanly style. But refine as you will, you cannot indulge in this luxury and not offend against the laws of decent society. If a man "chews" he *must* spit, and expectorated tobacco-juice *must* be nasty. You might say, naturally enough, " Why not use the spittoons ?" Impossible—they would be swamped in no time. There are plenty of dark and dirty corners in the halls and passages of every hotel, where, in the centre of a nauseating triangle of deep brown splashes and greasy blotches of black, you will find a brown earthen vessel sustaining an ill-directed fire of reddish fluid from the thousand passing throats ; but plentiful as these vessels are they are quite unequal to the demand.

So the Yankee makes a spittoon of every floor upon
which he stands. No matter of what material it consists, carpet or marble, he *must* spit. From the pavement in the street within a dozen yards of the front
door to the passages in the attics, the steps, corridors,
and staircases are one vast uncivilised pigsty. You can
hardly find a man in one of whose cheeks you will not
see a protuberance like the nuts in a monkey's jaw;
you cannot watch his mouth for two minutes without
observing a brown streak flying from it in amongst the
boots of the bystanders. You converse with one of
these biped cuttle-fish, and it makes no difference in
the activity of his bronchial muscles; enter into conversation with two or three of them, and you will have
to keep it up under a cross fire of murky jets squirted
across your face, over your shoulder, between your legs,
over your hat—everywhere, in fact, within a bare inch
of your person, as if you were standing up to a performance of the Chinese juggler's impalement. But I
must give the Yankees credit for being a match for any
of our Wimbledon shots; their oral accuracy of aim is
really surprising, and, like the Indian's skill with his
bow, only to be accounted for by constant practice,
following upon early education in the art, and juvenile
experiments upon flies on the walls. And if the sight
of all this nastiness is offensive to the eye, the unman-
nerly noises by which it is accompanied are even more
nauseous to the ear. Some of these fellows will retch

6

and hawk in such a way that you would think they would spit themselves inside out; no weak-minded patient, under the influence of an electro-biologist's evil eye, could be more demonstrative in his efforts to get rid of the fancied poison.

But I dare say you will be wondering how the ladies put up with all this beastliness.   They do not; they have a separate establishment of their own—a separate entrance, separate drawing-rooms, separate staircases in every hotel.   They could not associate with the majority of the men whose habits are so diabolical, so they sit, go out, and come in by themselves, except in the case of husbands and wives, brothers and sisters, and so on, in which cases, of course, a man is admitted to the ladies' drawing-rooms; not that he is imperatively excluded under other circumstances; but it is unusual for a gentleman unattended by ladies to venture into the sanctum of the fair sex.

This reminds me of a curious feature I have frequently observed in the manners and customs of this people, which is, the unjust preference given at all the railways, steamboats, and hotels to any man who can claim any sort of connection with any member of the opposite sex who will give him her protecting wing.   I have remarked on the unfair advantages given to the weaker sex themselves, and now I must tell you of the still more unjust privileges which are conceded to men who are taken to be travelling with them.   In England

and on the continent of Europe we are accustomed—I cannot deny it—to look upon the presence of a female companion as a drawback to the facilities of comfortable locomotion; but here I can assure you that a bachelor has a hard time of it, unless he has skill or impudence enough to attach himself to the skirt of some guardian angel. If you do not mind doing a bit of Yankee smartness, you can easily manage to represent yourself as "compagnon de voyage" to some fair or unfair protector. I am not particular to a т in a matter of this kind; the system is so absurd that I consider myself justified in resorting to any low artifice that may tend to demonstrate its folly; so I have constantly tried some impromptu dodge of practising an imposition upon the railway conductor, or the steamboat steward, and several times with complete success. With some officials the doing of a little light porterage in the way of a shawl or a dressing-case I have found to be quite sufficient to identify me as "belonging to that lady." With one it was necessary to do some heavier work and carry a very dirty disagreeable baby for an ugly ill-dressed mother, before I could induce him to give me a berth as "one of the party." It is a scandalous system altogether. Even granting that the females ought all to be accommodated first—a matter upon which I have my doubts—I see no principle whatever upon which the same privileges are to be extended to any loafer who passes himself off as in any way connected with them, in preference to a man who may have been waiting twice as long for a place, but unfortunately happens to be alone and honest. While the rule is so easily evaded, it is perhaps not so great a hardship, for the people are extremely free and easy, and you have no difficulty in getting into conversation with any one ; but, at the same time, I object very much to the bother of constantly dressing myself in false colours, and I have had serious thoughts of hiring some old woman to travel with me through the West. Any specimen of her sex would do equally well—an old nigger, even, I think would pay—and next time I visit this extraordinary country I must find some means of making a more satisfactory provision for the evasion of this extravagant rule.

I do not know that I have anything particular to say about the city of Chicago itself. As I said before, all American cities repeat themselves, like the Chinese. You know, of course how it lies, on the south-west corner of the Lake of Michigau ; and you have heard how the streets that now contain nearly 300,000 inhabitants were less than thirty years ago, open prairie. Never, I suppose, since the birth of history has a new town sprung to life with more marvellous, fairy-like rapidity, than have the stone and marble edifices that compose this great mushroom city of the plain. To walk through the broad handsome streets and inspect the lofty buildings on either side, and then to think that twenty-nine years ago there were scarce a dozen shanties on the spot, is to attempt to realise a thing so difficult of comprehension, that the mind becomes sceptical and refuses to believe it. But so it is; and if you consider for a moment the site on which the city stands, the head of the vast central plain of the North American continent, a region of natural fertility elsewhere unmatched; its facilities for water communication with the Eastern States and Europe; its position, the focus to which converge the lines of railway from all parts of Illinois and Indiana, from Wisconsin and Iowa, States which constitute the richest district of this agricultural wealth; the long neglect of these natural resources, and the rapid development now consequent upon their discovery; it becomes easier to understand how it is that Chicago has thus rapidly become, what it now is, the greatest primary grain depot in the world, the fountainhead of the vast stream of commerce which passes round the great lakes down the St. Lawrence, bearing the bountiful produce of the Western States to the markets of Europe. The city is, in fact, what the Democrats would have it recognised to be, the capital of the Western States; and I think the day is not far distant, though farther off than the English journals imagine, when Chicago and St. Louis—a city whose progress has been equally astounding—will be pitted in all the jealousy of a struggle for election to the honour of

being the commercial metropolis of a Western Confederacy.

On Sunday I attended service at the fashionable
church, a very fine one—the churches in all these
new cities are handsome and abundant—and heard a
most eloquent sermon in the style of Dr. Goulburn,
and music, such as I never heard at any other place
than Exeter Hall, performed by four professionals,
whose singing was the most delightful specimen of
sacred harmony that the most critical ear could wish
to listen to.   The rest of the day was spent in prome-
nading the town. Sunday is not well observed, for the
foreign element in the city is enormous; and those shops
that do no business on the Sabbath open their doors
and windows, so that to the eye of a careless observer
the trade might seem to be as lively as on any week-
day.   There was a violent storm raging on the lake,
which agitated the waters just as much as I have ever
seen them troubled in the English Channel, and the
promenade by the lake shore was consequently deserted
for more sheltered quarters of the city. But we walked
to the end of it, just to get a view of some of the
magnificent houses that have lately been erected
on the lake shore by the more lucky of the great
grain speculators of Chicago—splendid mansions many
of them, of red freestone or white marble, adorned with
greenhouses, creepers, and standard vines, worthy
residences for English peers, though lightly spoken of
as "summer boxes" by the nobodies who have screwed

a fortune out of this wretched war, and cannot get rid of it fast enough, with all the gambling and extravagance of this precocious city.

One peculiarity about the majority of the buildings, characteristic of the gigantic scale upon which, like the Egyptians of old, the Americans love to work, is the fact that they have been bodily raised in blocks of ten to forty or fifty houses at once from the original level at which they stood. The city was apparently run up in such reckless haste that the question of drainage was entirely forgotten, and it was not until successive inundations of the basement floors, which then stood below the level of the lake, warned the inhabitants of their precarious and unhealthy situation, that the attention of the architects was seriously called to the necessity for a change. English eyes, so they tell me here, would have seen no other way out of the difficulty than to pull down the whole city and reconstruct it on a higher level. But Yankee smartness knew a trick worth two of that, and with a bold defiant determination to outstrip all the wonders of the Old World, and " whip its engineers out of their boots "—a Yankee simile which you would better appreciate, if you were to see the great ponderous square-toed Wellingtons worn by the true American citizens, and the difficulty they have in getting into or out of them—conceived the original idea of lifting the whole city bodily into the air, and, by the aid of powerful screws and other " Yankee notions," it is now a *fait accompli.*

V.

CHICAGO.

Toronto,

September 15th.

The next day was wet, cold, and uncomfortable. I do not believe in climate; it is a failure everywhere. People point here to their blue skies and clear atmosphere, and tell you they " guess you do not see anything like that at home," under the impression that the sun is a sort of illuminated plane, of which we in England only see the wrong side. But I frequently have the honour of explaining to them that " November fogs" are not usual in July and August; and that malarious fevers, which result from the fearfully sudden changes of the American climate, are incidents of a rarefied atmosphere which " the Britishers" would be unwilling to take in exchange for their dull leaden skies and equable temperature. The fashionable disease here is not gout, but biliousness. There is a bilious look about everybody's face that makes the whole nation pale and yellow as children at the game of snapdragon

—a jaundiced gamboge in the visages of the men, that makes me think they must have swallowed the gold that has so mysteriously absented itself from the public gaze in favour of the countless raids of green-backs with which the country is overwhelmed. But, barring their sallow looks and yellow-ochre tint of countenance, these Western men and women are a marvellously fine race. Their frames are tall, well pro-portioned, symmetrical, and wiry. The average height of the men is astonishing. I have walked for hours in the streets of Chicago without meeting a native as short as myself. Most of their hats are almost out of sight—if I were shortsighted, would be totally. The women are tall, though not gawky, yet not exactly elegant. I have not yet decided where the defect lies, but there is something wanting somewhere. I think it is in the walk, which is rather duck-like, with an affec-tation of " sail" or " sweep" that looks " stagy." A little more rotundity of form to take off the corners would be required by an English connoisseur; but Yankee girls, like the men, are not given to lateral extension —they grow like poplars rather than pollards. Square and angular, however, though they be, all praise is due to their cast of features, which is in every case more or less classical, in some really beautiful. The cheek-bones are too high, the eyes too deeply set, particularly in the men, to make the full face represent the perfect type of beauty, but I am sure that no other nation that I know anything of could show so large a proportion of fine profiles. I have looked diligently for an ugly face—by which I mean one that has no features at all, such as we often see in England, and is known as the genus "college bed-maker"—but I have not been able to discover one that might not at least be considered passable. The percentage of good-looking people is undoubtedly far higher in America than it is at home, though the percentage of "beauties" is as certainly less. But the good looks are temporary, as you have often heard. Beauty fades in this climate as prematurely as the leaves fall from the trees. But its early death is not all due to atmospheric influences; it is a constitutional decay. Englishwomen will, in some cases, retain out here their youthful looks, long after their contemporaries of the Yankee tribe have buried theirs in sallow sunken cheeks, and hollow eyes, and toothless angular jaws—just as I observe some English trees in the public gardens fresh and green as in early spring, while their American brothers around them are already putting on their autumn dress. This is one view of the American "constitution" which to a medical man must be very interesting. I do not profess to account for it. Climate is a large element in this shortlived youthful freshness, this premature aridity of the vital fluids; but sweets, pie-crust, and iced water immoderately indulged in from the cradle to the grave, have, I suspect, as much to do with it. Yet it is a matter of national interest; for it is an acknowledged fact that if the population of the United States were left to the natural increase of the pure American blood, the census would never justify the confident expectations of the people as to their marvellous numerical growth.

But I have no time to tell you how surprised I was to find the American character so radically different from the English—how numerous are the points in which this great diversity consists. I am at a loss to know how to give you any idea of the general impressions I have formed of the Western people of this Continent, but I think they may be briefly expressed by saying that, physically, the men and women are Scotch, with French heads; intellectually, they are educated Japanese; socially, they are French without manners; morally, they are Spaniards without romance. In a word, they are un-English. The Continental European element enters largely into their composition. One-fourth of the shops in certain quarters of Chicago bear German names and signs. Immigration daily adds to the kettleful of nationalities, and climate warms the blood of the Anglo-Saxon ingredient; so the Western settlers become, like other inhabitants of the same parallels of latitude all the world over, hot, peppery, choleric, impulsive, foolishly impatient of anything that the most sensitive of Heidelberg duellists could distort into what be calls an insult

to his honour, inflammable in the company of females
as a lion or a bull. They tell me that pistols and bowie-
knives are not so ruthlessly employed as they were four
years ago. The war has diverted men's passions into
another channel, organized and concentrated them in
a direction in which they can have full play ; so that
travellers by the Mississippi boats have given up the
good old practice of sitting down to "whist" and
"euchre" with revolvers beside them on the table,
and street murders are almost out of date. But there
is still a marvellous recklessness of human life and
Lynch-law atrocities. Every day since I have been
in the West I have read in some paper or other a
paragraph or two, or more, recording the summary
shooting of some fancied enemies. Here is one
casually culled from a daily chronicle of the incidents
of life in New York.

"An officer was shot last night while defending a woman from
ruffians.

"A Mr. Burnett was shot while attempting to secure a burglar,
caught on his premises.

"A woman named Catherine Smith was shot through a window of
her residence in Second Avenue.

"A fireman named James Cornes was shot on the corner of Thir-
teenth Street and Fifth Avenue.

"Martin O'Connell was shot on the corner of Stanton Street and
Bowery.

"The above is a partial chapter of crimes in this city last night."

The climax is always introduced by a statement

that the victor "drew"—not, "*a*," but "*his* revolver," as if a pistol were as naturally to be found in a man's pocket as his handkerchief. No legal consequences seem to follow this promiscuous use of "repeaters." There are no police to take notice of it, or, if there are, they will be "mum" for a "cocktail." Persons with whom I have talked tell me they make a practice of carrying one of these civilising emblems of the westward march of Christianity. Sometimes I have had this humiliating confession from the mouth of a well-educated "high-toned" gentleman; at others, from the lips of daredevil youngsters, who seemed very incredulous of my assertion that my only weapon of offensive warfare was a tooth-pick. One gentleman told me he carried a pistol merely as a protection against the soldiers, with which the country now swarms; but I have never found any of them so thirsty after English blood as the 'New York Herald' would indicate. Now and then I have had to listen to brilliant invectives against the despotisms of Europe, and the British Government in particular (for Britishers are looked down upon by a Yankee as perhaps the most overridden of all the Continental peoples); but I have bitten my lips and held my tongue, and being, I consider, tolerably slow to wrath, I have managed without much difficulty to keep my skull unriddled with slugs. Besides, I feel confident that it is by no means necessary to get into any such scrapes. It is easy to avoid the "bars," where, in nine cases out of ten, these little "affairs" originate; and if you are unfortunate enough to impress a native so favorably as to lead him to demonstrate his liking for you by requesting that you will join him in "a drink"—it is his invariable method of showing his fancy, and refusal is instant death,—a very small amount of tact, and a moderate capacity for suction, will keep your friend's right arm quiet. But the evil is fast dying out, and, when the country becomes settled again, will, I dare say, become as much a thing of the past as the duelling of the Bois de Boulogne. Four years of civil war have so disturbed the machinery of the law, and unsheathed the evil passions of men, that it is the height of Utopian absurdity to come out here looking for a millennium. Still, the fact remains that the administration of justice must be very imperfect, if every one is compelled and allowed to take the law into his own hands.

This brings me to say a word about the Courts and their eccentricities, which very much shocked my English notions of judicial decorum and etiquette. The City Hall, in which the Courts sit, is a handsome building in an open square. The entrance hall and staircases are finished off in a style corresponding to the grandeur of the exterior, and in any other country than in Western America would be pleasant and airy lounges; but the marble floors are chequered with dark-yellow blotches, and intersected with brown streams, in which float ends of cigars and used-up quids of tobacco, and the windows are all shut down as if from fear that the effluvia from this Augean stable might poison the whole city; how I wished for a pair of pattens, and a very bad cold! The Courts were not yet sitting, but the crowd led me into a large well-lit neatly-furnished chamber, in which was to come on that morning a heavy case of libel. There were no benches or desks in front of the judges' seats; but an open semicircular space, sprinkled with little settlements of chairs, upon which were seated, in earnest conversation, the lights of the Chicago bar. Under the judges' seats was a table with pen and ink upon it, about as many papers as might be seen at home on a ten-days-old barrister's table, and about half-a-dozen square-toed boots, whose owners were finishing their post-prandial cigars, and spitting at a collossal reservoir that might have been a spittoon of the Titans. Nearer the door, and separated from the semicircle by an elegant iron railing, were commodious benches for the public, in one of which, after a careful search for a clean place for my boots, I sat down for a survey of the scene.

I waited some minutes, but nothing seemed likely to be commenced, so I asked when the judge would come into court.

"Oh, he has been here some time; that is him

in the white wide-awake, with his legs on the iron railing."

"Indeed," I said, "who is he talking to?"

"Oh, they are two of our great lawyers; that one that spat just then, is to be our next new judge."

"Well," I said, "how long will the judge keep us?"

"I guess he won't be long, he always has a bit of a chat first before he goes up into his *box*."

You may suppose from this conversation that my ideas of judicial etiquette were rather rudely shocked. Only think of our Master of the Rolls, or any other equally consequential, unbending occupant of our bench, chatting away with the bar and the clerks in the centre of the court preparatory to the business of the day! Fancy the Lord Chief Baron in shorts and a slouched hat, with a quid in his cheek, and his feet above his head, discussing the topics of the day with a knot of similarly-clad rowdies in a like horizontal position, and then, when he thought the public patience exhausted, clearing his throat with a roar that would have done credit to a lion, ascending his seat to take the business of the morning, and from his chair across the desk before him discharging his exhausted quid at the Brobdingnagian vessel of abomination that occupied the centre of the sacred semicircle. But this is just what you might have seen that morning in the chief court of the State of Illinois, and just, I suppose, what may be seen any day in that same polite assembly.

You might think, perhaps, as I did, that nothing could ever be done in such a chaos of anomalies as that; but here again is the great enigma of these Republican institutions. No sooner had the judge taken his seat than the work was begun, and pushed through with a rapidity and regularity that astonished me. Motions were taken and polished off in a way that would have horrified V.-C. Kindersley. There did not appear to be any books, or bags, or papers in the room. A small pocket memorandum was all that I could see in the hands of most of the barristers, while some did their work with the help of nothing more than a walking-stick. There was very little said; in fact, most of the business was transacted in a private whisper with the judge; each man, who had anything to "move," going up the steps and leaning forward over the side of the judge's desk, across which there flew a few hurried words, and the thing was done. There was no visible usher of the court, and yet there was no noise or confusion; no bags, wigs, and gowns, but yet a certain amount of rude unpolished etiquette; no dignity on the Bench, but a smart business-like decision which commanded respect. Indeed, I almost began to think that the abolition of our court paraphernalia would expedite the transaction of our business, and should have voted in its favour, only that just as the thought crossed my mind the judge aimed again at the spittoon, and back came all my loyalty to

7

our time-honoured institutions like a rush of blood
to the head. He could not have done that in a
wig.

The libel case came on shortly afterwards. It seemed
to be conducted much as it might have been at home.
The jury were sworn, as in Scotland, with the right
arm uplifted, and were addressed in a voluble speech,
which consisted chiefly of vulgar abuse of the opposing
counsel, who paced up and down the semicircle during
the delivery of the address, ever and anon venting his
wrath in a nauseating attack upon the spittoon. With
a powerful peroration the speaker wound up, and in an
instant his feet were on the table before him, and a
fresh quid was in his mouth. What was said in
answer to his attack I am unable to say, for the
atmosphere of the court was oppressive (the day being
very sultry), and a retreat was imperative. So we
fled from the presence of the law to that of a mysterious individual whose acquaintance we had made in the
cars, and who had asked us to come and call on him.
We found him in a little wooden cottage, crowded
with sumptuous furniture, and looking for all the
world like a pawnbroker's shop. Beside him was sitting, in costume that looked much more like a " chemise
de nuit" than a " robe du matin," a big bouncing York-
shire woman, whom he introduced as his wife ; and
the other occupant of the house was his son, who had
opened the door for us, a precocious young brat of

twelve, with a couple of gaudy rings. Mr. Knox himself, an expectorator of true transatlantic calibre, was
reclining upon a luxurious sofa, shoeless, coatless, vest-
less; smoking a magnificent cigar, and being fanned
by his wife. He was a smart clever man, and had
given us much information in the cars about the
country and the people, but had mystified us exceedingly about himself and his occupation. So we thought
we would pump him again, and thence came about our
visit. He had talked about the great coal-oil trade and
the Oil City of Pennsylvania, so we tackled him
about it, and he confessed that he had, till a few days
ago, been largely engaged in the trade; in fact, had
been one of the largest proprietors of the oil works;
but a little reverse had befallen him, and so he had
" executed a masterly flank movement" into the suburbs
of Chicago, where he intended to lie by for a few
months, and raise the wind for a fresh start in life.
He had been occupying an enormous house at the Oil
City, built with the money he had there made at a pace
which whipped all the incredible stories of the golden-
showered fortunes of San Francisco, and now he was
next to penniless; so he had packed up some of his
best furniture, and settled in this humble cot to retrench
a little before venturing into the speculating world
again.

Now, this case is one only of a thousand. Commercial gambling is carried on here to such a fatal

extent that a failure of this kind is thought as little
of as an attack of dyspepsia. " Some falls," we know
at home, " are means the happier to rise."   But here
I have heard it said that a man is not reckoned
" smart" till he has had a break-down, and " smartness," Anglicè dishonesty, is the highest trait in the
successful American's character.   The social ladder is
a sort of fire-escape, from the top of which a man may
slide to the bottom without damaging himself, and
find plenty of friends to help him up again : for credit
is cheap ; you can get it anywhere ; everybody will
take you on trust—a strange inconsistency of Yankee
nature which has struck me constantly on my travels—
and expect you to do the same in return ; and if you
do, be alive, for everybody lives on his neighbour, and
the least smart goes to the wall.   That was where we
found Mr. Knox just then, but he had a scheme in
hand for righting himself, and as it makes no difference
out here what a man *was*, to the public, who look only
to what he *is*, it mattered not that the line of specu-
lation he was about to try was as remote from that in
which he had failed as the two poles. What it actually
was he kept within his breast ; but it might have been
anything on earth that ever brought a man in an
honest or dishonest penny. A lawyer will come to
grief and turn tailor, a banker will stop payment and
become " a traveller," a shoe-black may fail and take to
politics and be a cabinet minister. No questions are

asked about the past; bygones are unreservedly bygones; family stigma is as little regarded as ancestral
respectability. Every American citizen, like the meanest
of French corporals, carries a marshal's bâton in his
knapsack. "Non quis, sed quid?" is the question put
to every one, the test of merit, the principle of reward.
Parentage, pedigree, lineal superiority, are disregarded.
Integrity gives place to "smartness;" social position to
unscrupulous ingenuity. Good stock is a weight upon
a man's back, beneath which he can rarely struggle
against the immigrant upstarts from the East, and not
be beaten in the race. Good blood is a curse to a
man, that brings down on his head, in language
more violent than that of John Bright or any other
platform demagogue, all the foolish prejudices and
savage denunciations of these enemies of what they
call "European aristocracy." So the men of real
worth are kept below the surface by the mushroom
nobodies that are always coming to the top like the
stones on a ploughed field, to be removed perhaps as
quickly, but only in favour of other "shoddy" more
pushing and unscrupulous than themselves. The social
scale has become inverted. Man is looked upon as a
mere machine of so much dollar-making power; and no
matter what the internal economy of the works, the
productive capacity is the only thing regarded. And
he that makes the largest amount of money (I cannot
say "income," for commercial success is not stable or

durable enough to permit men here to talk of annual
" incomes"), he that fills the biggest coffers with the
greatest rapidity and ease is the smartest, the best
man.

All this was well explained to us by Mr. Knox himself. He made no secret of the thing. He detailed
to us one or two of his smartest tricks in the short
years of his commercial life, and propounded to us
others that were then brewing under his presiding care ;
and so confident was he of his eventual success that he
invited me over to see him this time next year, in a
mansion twice as large as that he had just quitted ;
and I felt very much inclined to accept his offer, just
out of curiosity to see what can be done in this
wonderful country by that most original of all virtues,
Yankee smartness.

Well, I must not write any longer on this theme.
Our stay in Chicago was a very amusing one, for we
dived into every corner of the city, in order to see
every phase of Western life. But of course there are
no objects worthy of description in the smaller streets,
nothing like the picturesque poverty of an Italian
town, or the plain naked pauperism of London. Some
of the larger thoroughfares are still unfinished, for the
city is in its infancy, and in those there yet remain a few
wooden châlets, which will in a short time give place
to white marble blocks, like those that already stand
around them. The city officers have already inter-

dicted the erection of any more wooden houses, to ensure the safety and magnificence of the town ; and ten
or fifteen years hence, when the great streets are all
complete, and every building is fronted with marble,
Chicago will be as grand a city as any on this continent.

From the top of the lantern turret of the Court
House there is a splendid view of the city and the
suburbs, with the lake and the prairies on either side.
And on this balcony, while enjoying the prospect, I
had an interesting conversation with a very dirty-
looking individual, whom I should have taken to be
conductor of a London "penny 'bus." But no,
he was a colonel in the United States army, lately in
command of a negro regiment in Sherman's force.
His history was a curious one, by his own account, for
he had served three years in the army, half of the
time with the Confederates, and half with the Federals.
He was the son of a small Southern planter, enlisted
in the Southern army against his will, and getting
tired of eighteen months' short rations and hard work,
he had volunteered his services to the North, and
donned the light blue trousers and dark blue coat of
the Federal troops. His conduct seems to have been
so much admired that he was forthwith put in command of one of the negro regiments; and having been
in the habit of managing slaves in the South, he got
his regiment into a high state of efficiency, and, accord-

ing to his story, did wonders with it. But what impressed this conversation on my mind was the sickening tale he told of the inhuman barbarities practised on the field wherever his black regiment was engaged. Prisoners slaughtered, bodies mutilated, wounded men deliberately carved to death, as in the most horrible legends of Chinese executions, no quarter given, none asked—all this, and more than I had read in the English newspapers, was fully corroborated by his story.

I can well understand the exasperation of the South at the arming of the emancipated slaves, but really the tales that I hear of Southern cruelty and bush-whacking lawlessness, *allowing for the falsity of nine tenths of what I am told,* leave me in the gravest doubts about the justice of my Southern sympathies, with which I undoubtedly sailed from England. I am well aware that I am seeing only one side of the question, but the Democratic party of the West have a fair appreciation of the other, and from them I think I can get with tolerable accuracy at the statement of the opposite side. I do not intend to wheel round and turn Northerner, without cause or reason; but you must not be surprised if I come home with my ideas of Southern chivalry considerably modified. I will only say that I have not made up my mind about it at present, and shall not without consideration. At any rate, I cannot possibly entertain such respect for the

North as would lead me heart and soul to espouse their cause, but, at the same time, I am unable to discover those nobler points of character which had enlisted my sympathies on the Southern side ; so that I am inclined to be and talk neutrality ; and, with all due deference to the thunders of the 'Index,' and the conscientious opinions of the able men who conduct it, I must at present decline to go with them without further inquiry. And this I find no easy matter. The question is so complicated that every one I talk with looks at it in a different light, and has a fresh solution for the difficulty. It seems to me to be very little understood at home, and less, I sometimes think, here. But I am trying to get at the bottom of it, and if I ever do I will tell you what I think upon the subject. Till then, you and all readers of the 'Index' may consider me simply neutral.

Our friend in blue had occupied so much of our time with his voluble yarns about the war—in the course of which he related with much satisfaction how he had been the providential means of hurrying out of the world an equal number of Federals and Confederates in the course of his creditable career—that we had little time to walk down to the wharf and look over one of the famous " elevators " that have made the fortunes of so many Western grain merchants. I have no time to describe its operation ; but you may imagine the ingenious economy of time and labour

gained by the working of these elevators when I tell
you that the largest vessel that plies upon the Northern
lakes can be unshipped of its load of grain (which is
carried in bulk) in the course of a few hours. The
vessels draw up under the walls of these gigantic
buildings, and into the hold is thrust a great ele-
phantine trunk, which sucks up the loose grain to the
topmost story of the house. There it is cleaned, and
winnowed, and sorted, and in a few minutes down it
comes again through several pipes, according to its
quality, into the railway trucks that draw up to receive
it at the back of the building, and so it goes off to the
markets of the East. That which we visited was one
of the largest of all, an enormous pile of wood, looking
like an overgrown barn, or a very fine specimen of a
Pickford's van. It had three great trunks at work
upon the cargo of three grain ships, and a regular
depôt of trucks behind it receiving the grain, which it
rained forth in a host of golden showers. Inside all
was noise and dust. We threaded our way some distance through it to get a notion of the business going
on within, but the din stunned us, and the dust stifled
us, and we " skedaddled " into the open air again, more
bewildered than edified by our visit, and very hot and
peppery, looking for all the world as if we had been
racing in a flour sack, or pelted with " confetti " at a
Roman carnival. I cannot tell you how many of these
elevators there are along the quays of Chicago, but

their number is considerable, and their proportions are huge; and the sight of these in operation, with the busy aspect of the harbour, the river, and the wharves, would enable you to form some estimate of the vast grain business that has raised this city like magic from the prairie.

I do not know that I have anything else to tell you of Chicago, except that the mosquitoes are ten times as troublesome as any that I met in Malta. They do not seem to bother the natives, perhaps their blood is too bad to be worth the sucking, or else they are naturally mosquito proof; but the instinctive attentions of these insects to a stranger from the old world beat those of the most vigilant terrier that was ever set to welcome visitors in a yard. But it is no joke to receive too much of their attentions, as I did on the first night of my stay in the city; and it is a dreadful waste of the precious hours that ought to be devoted to peaceful slumber to spend one fourth of them in clearing the mosquito curtains and the bedclothes of the almost invisible enemy. And shake the curtains and the counterpanes as you will, flip about your towels as you may, you are tolerably sure to leave in some hidden corner one of the most active of his tribe, who will wait upon you as soon as you have tucked yourself up for the night, and considerately attend you till the day, trumpeting around your ears to announce his vigilance, as he looks out for a soft spot to settle upon, where the skin is thin and the blood is abundant. And though I am not given to spirituous liquors, I find the place which suits them as well as any other is the extremity of my nose. Yes, mosquitoes are the bane of every hot climate. The more I travel the more convinced am I that Dr. Hooker is right, in pronouncing climate to be "a failure everywhere." But there are other agencies of personal annoyance besides mosquitoes, and of all the worst are the flies. In England we are accustomed to look on a fly as a quiet, inoffensive animal, easily got rid of when not wanted; but here he is quite another character—the most impudent, brazenfaced, shameless ruffian you can imagine. He does not care for shakes of the head or fillips with a handkerchief one atom. You must deliberately pluck him off the feeding-ground on which he has billeted himself. Midges in the Scotch Highlands are nothing to these abominable flies. No article of food is safe for a moment from their attacks. Every morsel in your plate has an army encamped upon it, which throws out a batch of skirmishers over the mouthful you have cut and are just raising to your lips. Every dish has to be protected as best as it can be by a defensive screen of fine wire gauze, which completely hides the delicacies within, and makes you feel as if you were sitting down to dine off a lot of black fencing-masks. Truly, that fourth plague of old must have fearfully troubled the Egyptians.

VI.

THROUGH THE WEST.

CORNWALL;

September 22nd.

I HAVE been wandering some way from my subject, and I think it high time to find out my bearings before I am quite lost in the maze of innumerable matters of which I might sit and write had I time and inclination; so I will endeavour to take up again the missed trail, and tell you what I saw on my way to the Mississippi.

We left Chicago for the city of St. Paul, Minnesota, on the morning of September 6th. The journey occupied nearly three days—one in the cars to La Crosse, where we struck the Mississippi, 250 miles from Chicago, and thence 200 miles up the river by steamboats to St. Paul. Our railroad journey was marked by no particular incident beyond the death of a couple of cows run over by our engine on the track; but that is an everyday occurrence in this country; so much so, that every engine is armed with an ingeniously

contrived, plough-shaped machine, called in Yankee
parlance a "cow-catcher," which "catches" up all
stray cows and other animals that may happen to be
unconsciously blocking the way, and either impales
them on its iron apex or heaves them bodily aside
clear of the wheels. For hedges and ditches there
are none, and "snake fencing" even, for such tremendous distances as must be here enclosed, costs far
more than the companies can afford; so they ease
their consciences by stringing together a few loose
timbers here and there, as may be convenient, over
the least dilapidated of which the goutiest old cow
could leap with ease; and, beef being cheap, a very
moderate outlay in hush-money will shut the mouth
of any irritated farmer. As, then, every London
sweet-shop has its inevitable "fly-catcher," so every
American en-gine (it rhymes to red wine) has its inseparable "cow-catcher." It is so arranged that the
contact of the catcher with the body to be removed
causes no serious concussion, such as to throw the
cars off the track, or indeed do more than give you a
gentle hint that "there goes another cow." On the
occasion of which I am speaking nothing more was
perceptible than a very slight shock, which the natives
recognised instantly as "a cow;" and had it not been
for the remark of a neighbour, that he thought "there
must be two this time," I should have been quite
unconscious of what had happened, and never have

got out, when the train was brought to a standstill,
to see the mangled remains unspitted from the point
of the instrument.

The presence of this machine in front of the fore
wheels of every engine reminds me of another weapon
which takes its place in winter—the snow-plough, an
indispensable adjunct in the drifts, without which
locomotion would be an enigma. It is a very handsome, well-finished instrument, highly ornamental, and
when in action, I am told, its effect is really beautiful,
as it dashes away the snow on either side in a shining
silver shower. Indeed, the whole engine is a much
better-looking, better-cared-for institution than the
dull-green, smoke-dried machine, that nobody sits near,
if he can help it, on our English railways. In America it becomes an imposing, gay, gaudy monster,
decorated with flags and burnished brass, with a large,
handsome bell, which peals forth a merry "rondo" at
every crossing, every village or hamlet on the line, to
warn the inhabitants of its approach; and such a
whistle, too, as not all the professionals in sibilant
variations that occupy the gallery of "the Vic." on
boxing night could compete with for diabolical noises.
The only thing I know of capable of making a more
fiendish row than the whistle of an American railway
engine is the whistle of an American steamboat. To
the drum of a sensitive ear this latter is absolutely
excruciating; and if you ever have, what you are

pretty sure of having at some period or other during a
visit to this continent, a racking bilious headache,
you will thoroughly appreciate what I say. I am not
very particular on the subject of noises; any one who
has been thoroughly trained at school to learning his
morrow's repetition at one end of a room, while "high-
cock-a-lorum-jig-jig-jig" is going on at the other, does
not readily lose that acquired indifference to disturbing influences which Bass and Babbage are unable to
master. But the steampipes of the American boats
are intensely aggravating; far more worthy of par-
liamentary interference than the vilest compound of
heterogeneous discordance that ever was churned in a
barrel-organ. I should not mind even if they limited
themselves to one screech only at a time. They invariably belch forth three distinct sustained "whoops,"
with just interval enough between each two to allow you
to recover from the shock of the first, when the second
stuns you again. But I suppose one could get used to
the infliction, as one does to sermons and the income tax;
at any rate, the natives seem to like it, for they hurry
forth from every house to muster on each landing-stage
by the river side at the first note of the trumpet-
tongued siren; and there they gape and stare at the
hoarse monster (like the Trojans at the monster horse)
as she empties her living cargo upon the wharf, to such a
deafening bellow as all the wax that Ulysses stuffed into
his crew's ears could never have kept out of mine.

But this is a land of wonders, and steam-whistling is only one of them. There are plenty of other things that excite my astonishment, as I proceed on my travels amongst these wonderful people. I wonder why the boats and trains are all so crowded ; where the travellers come from, where they are going, that the traffic should be so incessant. I wonder how the boats steam so fast without blowing up more often than they do. I wonder how the trains run through the streets of the cities without frightening all the horses and killing all the children. I wonder how the boats all go without any visible captain, the trains without any tangible conductor ; how anything, in fact, goes right at all, where nobody seems to have the management of anything. I wonder why the toes of all the boots are square, as in the armour of the middle ages ; and how far up the body a Yankee's "Wellingtons" extend, seeing that the ordinary custom of tucking the trousers—I beg his pardon, "pants"—up to the knee discloses no termination of the leather casing. I wonder why these square-toed soles are always to be seen looking out of every window, and why you will invariably find a Yankee's feet where you would expect to find his head. I wonder whether pocket-handkerchiefs are forbidden by the Constitution, and where the Yankees got the notion that spittoons were intended as receptacles for ends of cigars, and nothing else. I wonder what chewing-gum is made of, and why the women

8

are never easy unless they are engaged in dissolving
that or candies. I wonder why there are no children
in the States, no girls or boys as in merry England,
but only immatured young men and women, *à la
Française,* without a particle of French *esprit.* I
wonder who is the master of a household, the embodi-
ment of the English " paterfamilias," seeing that the
mistress is as good as the master, and the meanest
" slavey," in her own estimation at any rate, better
than either. I wonder how it is that no one ever
laughs, or tries a joke or a pun but the President;
and dinner is a solemn feed, the gravity whereof must
be undisturbed by that delightful *badinage* of wit
and humour, which is the best served dish at an
English table. I wonder whether the Americans of
the East are at all like those of the West, and if so,
how it comes about that human nature has been able
to scrape itself so bare of the polish which old-fashioned
Europe supposes to be inseparable from education,
however superficial. I wonder why everybody com-
bines, with an almost Puritanical love for the inside
of a place of worship, such a barefaced disregard for the
third commandment as would excite the envy of the
most blasphemous of British bargees, and would have
" whipped " the vocabulary of the famous fishwoman of
Billingsgate as thoroughly as did the wit's retort that
she was a " parallelopiped." I wonder, indeed, at
everything I see and hear ; wonder, in fact, whether,

if I stayed here for the rest of my life, I should ever understand one jot the better this most marvellous of marvellous people.

Our route to the Mississippi ran across a tract of the great prairie country, in the centre of which the city of Chicago stands. Much of it has been settled and cultivated, and so the aspect of the land has been materially changed; but here and there, as the cars dragged along their heavy weight, with those excruciating jerks which would throw any but an American train off the track, it was possible to get some little idea of the scene which used to meet the eye when the hand of man had as yet been idle upon the surface of the soil, and far and wide as the sight could reach, the heaving waves of long rank grass rolled along to the music of the western breeze—not a tree, not a shrub to break the hardness of the dull even outline, not a sign of human life to relieve the monotony of the landscape, not a sound save the whiz of the prairie fowl's wings to tell that any life was there,—and stand wherever the traveller would, on any hillock or eminence he could find, he would see the horizon still bounded by the same green distance, and for days, as he pursued his journey, the sun would rise out of and sink into the same endless ocean of unvaried verdure. But people have "gushed" and poetised enough upon the rolling prairies of the West, and I, who have not seen them in their primitive glory, have no right to follow suit.　For myself, I must confess that I like variety of outline in preference to solemnity of repetition, picturesque irregularity rather than severe monotony, Kensington's ornamental waters far better than the open sea.

The country was drearily level.　The famous dun cow, which Ruskin saw above the distant horizon on his visit to Cambridge, would stand out sharper and clearer here, with less, if possible, to interrupt a full view of its proportions than in the vicinity of that mathematical focus.　Ever since I left Ottawa and Montreal, I have experienced most keenly that longing for a bit of swelling ground which used to drive the Cambridge undergraduates, when in "the blues" about the flatness of everything, to seek a view of those noted mole-heaps which cruel sarcasm calls the "Gog-Magogs."　I do not suppose anything is more likely to strike the traveller in the West than this wearisome evenness of the country. I noticed with disappointment the same feature, but less aggravated, in what I have at present seen of Canada.　Do not imagine that I mean to say that the ground is absolutely so painfully level as in the fen-country of the Eastern Counties of England, but there is nothing like a mountain about it, nothing which the wildest imagination, or the purest disregard for accuracy, could designate as a tenth-rate hill.　Trees, there were a few, further on towards the Mississippi, where the railroad struck again into straggling remnants of the old primeval forests; and ever and again some indication of the many settlements that are rapidly springing up from the ground to take the place of the tangled brushwood so fast disappearing before the torch of the Anglo-Saxon. Towns too we passed, busy centres of incipient wealth and prosperity, where was going on a brisk trade in timber from the lately cleared forests, and where, I doubt not, a few years hence you would see a lively market for the grain to which the forests are giving place.

Bordering the track on either side, the country was for the most part already clear, and where so cleared it was divided into large fields partitioned off in parallelograms, by " snake fences" of split logs piled one above another, in a sort of zigzag pattern, without cord or tie of any kind. The generality of the fences seemed to be of this simple character, for all the world like those jointed penny rules or measures, that, as a child, I used to have the ill-luck to get off every Christmas tree. But some farmers, of less easy approach, have fenced their lots off from the encroachments of their neighbours, by laying side by side around their borders an army of roots and stumps of the trees cleared off their land. The points of the roots are turned outwards, without being cut off or clipped into any sort of shape, but there they are left to harden like iron, which they soon do under the influence of the dry atmosphere; and most curious is their appearance, and, to a huntsman, I should say, far more formidable than the thickest and tallest of Leicestershire "bull-finches," for they tower aloft, some of them many feet into the air, more irregular perhaps, than the bayonets of the most awkward squad of British Volunteers that ever claimed the Government subsidy, but presenting a *chevaux de frise*, that no cattle or trespassers could penetrate, without the respective loss of hide or nether garments.

The corn, which on this continent means exclusively Indian corn, in contradistinction to wheat, was in many places up and stored—it is never stacked—when we passed along the road; for it ripens with marvellous rapidity, attaining its full height of ten and twelve feet, and in Kentucky even more, in the short space of three months. In some places, however, we came across farms where the harvest was going on, and the farmers were levelling the huge corn-stalks, of almost sugar-cane height and substance, with heavy two-handed sickles that reminded me of Turkish scimitars. In other places we passed through patches of corn of later growth, still ripening for the harvest, with pumpkins and water-melons upon the ground beneath it, interspersed with the stalks. The abundance of these fruits is marvellous; they grow everywhere and anywhere, and when the inhabitants of the country have stuffed themselves with all they can digest—and the amount they do digest is astonishing

THROUGH THE WEST. 119

—they turn the cattle into the fields to finish them, and wouldn't it shock the nerves of the Jewish merchants of Covent Garden, to see the beasts revelling in fruit that would do credit to any English dessert ? I wonder if I shall ever have the heart again to stump up to those nosey grocers the exorbitant price they demand for such a melon as I have seen a cow eat for nothing.

Whilst upon the subject of melons and pumpkins, let me say that the vegetable productions of this continent, and the vegetarian tastes of the natives, are, to an Englishman, who rarely sees any other accompaniment to his roast beef than potatoes and horse-radish, matters of constant astonishment. In the first place, there is the sweet potato, the original potato I suppose, from which ours is to the Yankee mind a degenerate descendant. But I do not at all agree with that view, and have, I suspect, all Ireland with me in my opinion, though I have had several encounters upon the subject with certain obstinate waiters, who persisted in bringing me the sweet genus in preference to the ordinary kind. Indeed, it is necessary to specify the latter as "common potatoes;" and much as my feelings revolt at the application of so humiliating an epithet to what I consider, without doubt, the finest vegetable ever invented, I find it the only way of insuring its presence on my table. Then there is the egg-plant, served in slices fried, first rate ;

squash, a sort of vegetable marrow, mashed, and succotash, something like it, both very decent; hominy, apparently grains of the Indian corn in a compound of butter; and the inevitable tomatoes, always pronounced "tomaytoes," as necessary to an American at his dinner as his iced-water, and that is absolutely indispensable. Then there is the green Indian corn boiled into a yellowish white, which everybody eats before the pudding, first besmearing it with butter, and then holding it to his or her mouth, as the case may be, with both hands, and, as it rotates upon the two forefingers, gnawing the grains from the stalk, like a rat nibbling round the wick of a candle. The process for a lady is an inelegant one, but I do not know that there is any other mode of consumption; for the corn is of too tough a texture to cut, and the grains are too firmly implanted in the little cavities of the stalk in which they grow to allow them to be detached by a fork or spoon—and they pass out into your mouth so easily when you apply your fore-teeth to their sides, that I am quite certain they were intended to be so eaten.

Add to those that I have enumerated, every vegetable that we have at home, and you will not wonder at the surprise of the nigger, who waited on me at my first hotel dinner, when I innocently ordered "vegetables," and to his necessary demand, "What vegetables?" as innocently answered, "Whatever there are," utterly

unconscious of the prodigious results of what seemed
to me a most natural order.   But my neighbours were
not half so amazed at the preposterous number of
small dishes by which my order was followed up as
you might have imagined.   No American sits down
to his meat without at least half a dozen vegetables,
all on separate saucers, and all going at once; for he
has them arranged all round his plate, and dives into
them promiscuously, as the particular. mouthful he is
engaged upon may seem to require one or the other;
and therefore, if, instead of half a dozen, I had a dozen
and a half of these small saucers round me, no one
thought it particularly extravagant. If any eccentricity
on my part surprised any one, it was that I did not
consume the whole of them.

We passed for many hours through various scenes
of farming life in the West.   In a few cases through
moderate-sized farms, in most through lately settled
lots, where the virgin soil was in every stage of
gradual adaptation to the presence of civilised man.
Here, the fields were already laid out and fenced off,
but the stumps of the felled trees were still in the
ground, blackened with the fire annually applied to
them, to deaden their vitality, and loosen their hold
upon the soil, until, in the fourth or fifth year, they
could be bodily uprooted from their matrix.   In the
mean time grass had been sown around them, òr scanty
Indian corn, but in general the forest had been so

thick that little space was left between the scarred and
crumbling stumps.   Here, the trees had been lately
felled, and their trunks were lying about the ground
in confusion picturesque enough to gladden an artist's
eye.   There, some new comer had just fired the
forest, and goodly giants of pine and oak and beech
were being charred to ashes by the flames, in a reckless waste that would have vexed the spirit of an
English landowner.   But wood is so abundant that
no one knows what to do with it, and inland carriage
far too expensive to make the export of it pay ; so
that, unless the farm be situated in the neighbourhood of some large stream, down which the timber can
be floated to the sea-board, the forest growth must be
destroyed on the spot.

The road throughout was novel, but after a time
monotonous.   The eye soon wearies of branchless
trunks and charred stems, alternating for miles and
miles with ploughed fields and snake or root fences,
without an undulation of the ground to relieve the
flatness of the country.   And as for the forests themselves, I did not see any striking peculiarity in the trees
or their size ; and, indeed, I was at first puzzled to see
that their growth was comparatively so diminutive in
a country which must have been overspread with wood
for ages.   But this is explained by the frequent occurrence of the conflagrations that rage through the
forests of these dry climates in the summer heats,

whose inroads play such havoc among the trees that a fifty years' growth of timber is almost a rarity. The real beauty of the American forests is only to be seen in the fall, when they clothe themselves in such a variety of autumnal tints as would make the gayest of English October foliage pale and dull beside them. But as yet the sun was hot, and Nature's autumn dresses in her wardrobe.

Before I take you to the Mississippi I should like to say a few words about the agricultural resources of the West, " the great West," as its inhabitants not inaptly call it. Not that I consider myself qualified to speak with any weight upon the subject, or wish you to imagine that I have any thoughts of setting myself up as an authority upon a matter of which you are sure I can have little knowledge. But we have all heard so much of the vast tide of emigration that is daily setting in to the shores of this continent on its way Westward to the great valley of the Mississippi, that you cannot suppose I have travelled through the country where these strangers from the old world are making their new homes, without picking up some information about the land of their choice; and what little I have thus learnt I think it my duty to transmit to you.

It must be conceded, I presume, by the most self-contented of British landowners that the present condition of the agricultural body of our people is pecuniarily inferior to that of any other class. Farmers, we know, are by nature and profession grumblers, but if you or I were as often victimized by the weather or the grub, we should be as bitter too, and farmers' grievances, now-a-days are by no means limited to eccentricities of the barometer, or the attacks of insidious entoma. So long as Great Britain continues to prosper, the value of land must increase, for there can be no increase of the land itself, and the farmer derives no benefit from the ever-growing competition for its possession. He has to compete not only with men of his own stamina and profession, but with others, who have made their money in other walks of life, and will pay for the advantages of a country re-tirement a price which is not measurable by the ordinary rates of profit. Then, with his rent raised by this continued competition, he has to meet in his own market the produce of foreign lands, whose purchase price is little or nothing, or rent perhaps as trivial. He has, of course, the cost of transport in his favour, but freight only balances the manure, without which his soil cannot be cultivated, and foreigners, whose land is rich enough to yield without manure, or extensive enough to render it unnecessary to expend upon it an equal amount of labour, can undersell him at pleasure. So the British farmer has turned dairyman, and the special adaptation of the soil for the rearing of stock has tended to modify the evil effects of foreign competition in corn. But, it is an undoubted fact, that the proportion between our producers and consumers of food is undergoing a rapid change. The manufacturing, mining, and town populations are fast absorbing the business of the country, and while the landowners' profits increase with the rising value of land, the area left for the farmer is diminished, and the competition for it proportionally augmented. Such, or somewhat similar, are the reasons, I fancy, which are inducing the present attempts to thin the ranks of home competition, by sending off the young and enterprising to some quarter of the globe where they can possess themselves of a fertile soil, and thence contribute to the wants of the old country, whose home resources are utterly inadequate to supply the mouths of her dense population.

Whither then to send them? No country, perhaps, offers greater inducements to the settler than the upper valley of the Mississippi. In few places, I suppose, can land be procured on more favorable terms than in the prairies of Illinois or the surrounding states. For instance, the Illinois Central Railroad Company are offering for sale more than a million acres on either side of their line, at prices varying, at the present rate of gold, from 12s. to 60s. an acre, on long credit, extending over a period of seven years. The soil, composed of a deep rich loam, bears analytical comparison with the most fertile organic deposits. It is generally so easily worked that the labour of one man is as effective as that of many on rockier soils, and far more productive. The natives have a saying that a man has nothing to do but "scratch the prairie with a fork" and it yields immediately; and the principle has been acted upon so largely, that settlers, who have never taken the trouble to plough more than an inch or two deep, have, in some instances, been led to doubt the truth of the representations upon which they were induced to settle here. But if proper attention be paid to the ordinary rules of agriculture, the fertility of the soil is inexhaustible. Some have much exaggerated the scarcity of wood and water, but the fact is that the Illinois prairies are studded with copses or groves, and though there may be no streams in their central districts, yet water can always be had at the depth of a few feet. Then the means of intercommunication provided by nature are boundless, in rivers whose navigable waters may be measured in thousands of miles, and lakes of which any one would drown the whole of the British Islands. And if the natural commercial facilities of the West are great, the artificial are rapidly assuming a corresponding magnitude. The Americans are too canny to be indifferent to the all-important influence of a railroad. They civilise with the steam-engine and the telegraph—the Bible is left to follow—and these two pioneers of civilisation are bringing in their wake an amount of worldly prosperity which, at any rate, seems to prove the pecuniary success of the principle.

To small capitalists, then, amongst our British farmers, who are weary of high rents, and little or no profit in the best of wheat seasons, so that it is actually a matter of doubt with some whether a bad harvest is not as profitable to the farmer as a fine one, seeing that the prices of a favorable year are knocked down by foreign competition to little above the sum realised by the scantier crop of a bad season—to the poor farm-labourers, struggling for bare existence with their wives and families upon the wretched pittance that is eked out to them as a remuneration for the sweat of their brow; seeing, perhaps, from year to year, no more of the meat which their labours have raised than the Christmas portion doled out from the squire's porch, and knowing no more of the significance of our boasted word "home" than can be divined within the narrow mud walls of mouldering hovels that have recently provoked the indignation of our philanthropists—let us hope for some good purpose—to all, in fact, who have fainted in the race that man runs with man for the prize of the bare means of sustenance, or have been jostled out by the crowd who are forced to compete in it, the prairie lands of the great West offer, as it seems to me, a wide field for enterprise, and a certain reward for energy. British soil has no doubt its own peculiar advantages—the happiest combination of liberty and order under its admirable political constitution; the most equitable, if complex, laws; the healthiest, if not the brightest climate; the most varied though quiet scenery; attractive enough each and all to those who can afford to live there and enjoy them. But Great Britain, though considerably more diminutive than many of the American states, attempts to support a population almost as large as that of the whole of the states put together. The vessel is awfully overcrowded, and some must go overboard to keep her afloat. Home, of course, has its charms, which must always stem the natural flow of emigration; but for a farm labourer of the present day to talk of home ties seems almost rhapsody without rhyme or reason.

If, then, the time has arrived when the poorer of our agricultural people must seek their bread elsewhere, why not invite them to the western prairies of America? There are, possibly, other countries which present equally good prospects to the agricultural emigrant. I venture to speak only of what I have seen and heard for myself. But here, at any rate, is the very field desired—a virgin soil of easy culture and extraordinary natural fertility, with little or no forest to clear, in a country traversed by the most perfect system of railways, where no settler need be more than ten miles from a station, whose shore is washed by one of those gigantic lakes, through

which an outlet is found to the Atlantic, and whose
rivers are providentially adapted to become vast ar-
teries of commerce in the very heart of the continent.
The soil is underlaid with coal and iron and lime.
There is a complete organization of markets ; an ever
increasing local demand for every article of agricultural
produce, and a constantly growing sale for exports ;
and all this within a fortnight's journey from our shores.
Seven pounds will set an emigrant from Liverpool
down in Illinois.   If he have not the required capital
to take a farm at once, three or four years' labour will
probably place him in funds to commence his career as
a proprietor of the soil ; and for the same sum as he
would have to pay as a year's rent at home, he may
become the absolute owner of, probably, better land here.
Manual labour is dear, but its price is economised by
the most extensive and profitable use of agricultural
machinery ; and horse-keep, at home so expensive, will
cost him little, while his stock will be free to graze on
the unoccupied prairie.   Are not such announcements
as these, which I have culled from conversation with
some of the settlers here, tempting enough to allure
the most dull of understanding ?   Is it not incredible
that, in the face of assertions like these, oft repeated
as they are by men of weight and authority, any should
wilfully prefer to stay at home and starve?   People
talk with amazement of the emigration that is so rapidly
thinning the population of Ireland ; but the wonder

9

with me rather is that any should stay behind at all.

I have not the least doubt that all who chance to read these lines will accuse me of base intrigues with Bright and Abraham Lincoln for entrapping my fellow countrymen into the ranks of the Federal army. But my conscience is clear on that point, and besides, I do not believe, as I shall tell you at greater length some day, that a hundredth part of the statements of the ' Times ' upon the last four years of American history, will bear investigation by an unprejudiced inquirer after truth. At any rate I have no inducement to launch out into these panegyrics of the Western States beyond a conscientious belief in the truth of what I have learnt on the spot, and a firm faith in the advantages of emigration, to the emigrant no less than to those he leaves behind him. The future of the great West cannot but be a grand one. The day of her greatness seems at the present moment far distant. But sooner or later the clouds that overshadow this Continent must clear. It is impossible for a foreigner to realise the progress of development up to the outbreak of the war, in the region northwest of the Ohio river. Seventy years have hardly passed since the first American colony settled there. Since then the changes that have taken place are such as the world has not seen elsewhere. Seven States carved out of the acquired Indian Territory—cities founded, one of which, Chicago, boasts a population of nearly 300,000, while others count their thousands in hundreds—towns and villages planted everywhere—forests levelled and converted into cultivated farms—railways and roads constructed—telegraphic communication established—lakes and rivers floating a perfect commercial navy. What the next seventy years will bring no one can pretend to foresee. Whether the hopes of some of my countrymen will be realised and the flag of a Western Confederacy float at Chicago, or whether that great city will still be playing second fiddle to the still greater metropolis of New York, I do not hazard a conjecture; but at least I think I may congratulate myself in having had the luck to get a passing glimpse into a country which is without doubt destined to play an important part in the world's history.

VII.

THE MISSISSIPPI.

BOSTON,

September 28th.

IT was one o'clock in the morning before our 250 miles of railway were accomplished, and La Crosse, our point of contact with the Mississippi, reached. It was then too dark to see anything of the great river whose waters we had come so far to look at, and the train was so full of passengers, that we had to make the best of our time in attempting to get places on the boat. The cars ran, of course, up to the water's edge, and by the wharf lay the steamer ready to receive the train's cargo. To our great disappointment the boat was not one of those far-famed denizens of the Mississippi, whose huge proportions and propensities to blowing up, are equally notorious in the annals of Western America ; but a very poor specimen of the shipwright's architecture, of extremely modest dimensions, and most uncomfortable passenger accommodation ; and for this unlooked for usurper of the

domains of the great river, we had to thank the
" Father of Waters" himself, who had been so reduced
by the long drought which had prevailed throughout
the summer, that none but the most insignificant craft
could pass his scanty shallows.   The rush for the few
berths that were to be had was thoroughly characteristic of the people.   It was entirely confined to the
" ladies "—a generic term which includes all the sex,
from the President's wife to the meanest white
" help "—and whilst they fought and clamoured
amongst themselves for the coveted luxury of a dirty
berth, the humbler representatives of the weaker sex—
the American idea of my own—waited with exemplary
patience outside, for the chance of what at school we
used to call the " scrapings." But the chance was infini-
tesimally small ; there were not half berths enough for
" the ladies," the steward told us, so I resigned myself
to fate and ingenuity to find a place for the night's
rest, and spent the few minutes we had before leaving
the pier in admiring the figures of two gigantic Indian
warriors who came on board the boat for whiskey and
cigars.

  They were noble specimens of humanity ; six feet
three or four in height as they stood in their woollen
socks, which served them for shoes. A coarse blanket
thrown carelessly over the shoulders, and a band
round the head with a few feathers in it, seemed to be
the only other article of dress with which they encum-

bered their toilet. There was no diffidence or shyness
about their manner, as they moved in and out amongst
the passengers; they carried themselves erect as worthy
representatives of the proudest of tribes, the great
Sioux—a tribe that has cost the American government
more trouble, money, and lives, than any other; the
very tribe in fact which has this summer broken out
again in the northern Mississippi, and to repress which
our boat was carrying up soldiers detached from the army
of Sherman. No doubt it was to spy out the number
and destination of these troops that the visit of the wily
pair was made, but their cool cunning and intrepidity
had secured them an easy admission to the steamboat
as friendly Sioux of the opposition party that disap-
proved of the late massacres perpetrated by their fellow-
kinsman in the North. I watched with interest their
quiet cat-like movements through the crowd, and, as I
looked at their features, I was immensely struck with
the theory I had heard of their affinity to the Mongol
or Tartar race—the same broad flat countenance and
high square cheek bones, the same tendency to oblique-
ness in the eye's position and form, the same long
straight black hair, the same copperish-yellow colour
of skin, that I believe to be the characteristic features
of those mysterious people.

As the whistle sounded, they moved sullenly off to
communicate, I suppose, the intelligence of what they
had learnt to their brethren in arms, and having

watched them off the boat, I seized one of the
mattresses that were being thrown promiscuously upon
the cabin floor, and there, in the midst of a Babel of
snorers similarly situated with myself, I contrived to
get as much sleep, as the incessant trampling of the
restless spirits who could not find a place to lay their
heads, and the noisy political discussion of those who
sat up to make a night of it, would admit of my
taking. But I was not let alone long. Before five
o'clock the black stewards hoisted the ends of the
mattresses and tipped out their occupants on to the
floor, and there I might have lain if I had liked,
as some few did with imperturbable "*nonchalance*,"
surrounded by niggers sweeping all over them, and
tumbling against their limbs, and setting tables across
their stomachs, and chairs and benches upon their legs,
only that I preferred to rise and look at the Mississippi;
and, having performed the most cursory of all
superficial ablutions, with a teaspoonful of water and a
square inch or two of unused towel, I rushed upon the
deck, and saw something after this fashion :

A broad expanse of extremely shallow water; a
number of oddly-shaped marshy-looking islands; a
tortuous channel in and out amongst them, very
difficult of navigation, and intersected by frequent
sandbanks, on the top of which the keel of our boat
grated at every other bend in the stream, with a dull
sound that brought home to the passengers the un-

comfortable apprehension of the possibility of sticking fast on one of these banks and seeing much more of the Mississippi than we had bargained for ; a low vegetation on most of these islands, very much like that which may be seen on any of the alluvial deposits on the Thames ; a range of steep bluffs on either bank rising abruptly from the water's edge, sparsely wooded and bare alternately, but bold in outline and precipitous.   Such was my first impression of the Mississippi scenery, and such it is now, for there was little or no variety, save where the line of the high bluffs was occasionally broken by a deep wild-looking ravine, in the shelter of which lay now and then a few farmers' cottages, and sometimes, but at long intervals, a village or a town.

There was an impressive sense of solitude forced upon me by the aspect of everything around ; a feeling of loneliness not even dispelled by the appearance of the small towns at which we called on our passage ; for, shut in, as they were, by the narrow gorges in which they lay, and debarred from communication with the outer world except by the shallow waters through which we were feeling our way, they seemed to me so many hermits' settlements ; each one, as it lay in the distance, promising to be the most advanced outpost of these lonely pioneers of civilisation, till another and another successively came in view, to testify to the fact that neither the solitudes of the prairie, nor the

darkness of the forest, can stem the advance of human
enterprise. Beyond these few detached settlers' colonies,
there was nothing to be seen indicative of the busy
life that must, no doubt, ere long, in the progress of
development of the great North-West, culminate
towards the waters we were traversing.   Besides our
own boat, none did we see, but her sister craft on the
downward passage, laden with recruits from the North
for Sherman's army.   A few rude looking "lumberers,"
at the various wood stations at which we called for
fuel, a few cows near the settlements, and a good
sprinkling of herons and kingfishers, the latter of a
brilliant blue, were the only varieties in the long
panorama of shallow water, marshy islands, sandy banks
and distant bluffs; and glad as I was to feel that I
was actually upon the great Father of Waters, I must
confess that my visit to his Majesty's presence disappointed me.   I ought, however, in candour to add,
that his unimposing aspect was in great measure due
to the unprecedented drought ; and that, had he been
rolling down his accustomed body of water, and
carrying his visitors comfortably housed in the floating
palaces which at ordinary times ride with ease upon
his surface, I should have come away with a far better
opinion of his right to his accredited position as the
Father of Waters ; as it was, he appeared to me very
much in the light of an impostor, and, as one of my
fellow-travellers observed, I think it extremely doubtful

whether, in his then state of aqueous insolvency, proud little Father Thames himself would have owned him even for a poor relation.

Well, as there was really so little to see outside the boat, or, at least, so little which it would interest you to hear of, I will turn your attention to that from which I myself derived more amusement—the boat itself and the passengers. In the first place, as to the boat. It was the queerest machine by which I had ever travelled. It had neither paddles nor screw, but an enormous water-wheel of the rudest construction, at the stern, worked by the most primitive of engines, which occupied the after part of the lower deck. Engine, furnace, fuel, and all, entirely above the water's level; for the boat drew but a few inches of water. The upper deck consisted of a sort of apology for a saloon, with a few boxes on either side, that answered the purpose of ladies' berths; and in a sort of balcony that ran round the outside of this deck, and on the roof of it, the passengers aired themselves upon a limited number of kitchen chairs and three-legged stools that formed the only furniture of the vessel. After staring for some time at the lazy movements of the great wheel, and deciding that the whole concern looked exactly like a locomotive water-mill, without the slightest pretensions about it of conformity to the ordinary lines upon which I had hitherto supposed it necessary to construct a boat, I studied the passengers.

The majority of them were soldiers, as I have already mentioned, on their way northwards to quell the outbreak amongst the Indians. Of the general appearance of the Northern army as yet I know but little. I shall have more opportunity of speaking on that point when I get to Washington and New York. Suffice it to say now, for the benefit of those who read nothing but the 'Times' and are content with what they there read, however great the internal evidence of its untruth, that they were not English, nor Irish, nor Germans, nor French, nor any but genuine Americans; farmers mostly, and farmers' sons, well informed on every point of common interest to the public at large, quiet and orderly to a degree which surprised me and my fellow-travellers from England. We mixed and talked with them with much pleasure, and gleaned from them what we could of their ideas about the prospects of the war. They spoke of the Southern enemy with no animosity beyond what they vented upon the large slave-holders, to whose machinations they attributed the co-operation of the poorer classes. What few expressions of ill-feeling they used were poured forth against the Southern women, whom some of them, who had come from New Orleans, declared to be perfect she-devils incarnate; and if but a few features in their portrait of a Southern woman be correct, I must admit that General Butler's task in that devoted city was no easy one; and, indeed, I should

feel much inclined to be ungallant enough to go
further, and say that the extreme measures to which
he resorted during his " Reign of Terror " were not
wholly unjustified. At any rate it is admitted by all
that much improvement in the domestic and sanitary
arrangements of the city has resulted from his un-
welcome dictatorship; and that what was formerly a
sink of pestilence and iniquity is now a decent and
well organized community. We talked of Grant and
McClellan, and found that the latter had completely
lost the ephemeral popularity that America vouchsafes
to her short-lived favorites.   " The young Napoleon,"
but a few months back the idol of the army, was now
rarely spoken of without a sneer. Grant, whose
highest quality in their eyes seemed to be his con-
descension in sleeping upon a private's blanket, was
now the darling of the day.   Should his long-looked-
for plunge into Richmond be much further delayed,
his name will be consigned without scruple or ceremony to the rack of obloquy and anathemas upon which
the North has annihilated so many of her transient
heroes. Sherman and Sheridan are also in the ascend-
ant. The reign of each promises to be a brilliant
one; the marvel of its brilliancy, perhaps, like the
meteor's, only to be equalled by that of its rapid
evanescence. Of all the generals that this war has
called into being, whether on the side of North or
South, Robert Lee is the only one who has retained

the place to which the chances of battle have raised
him.   But his military genius is undoubtedly superior
to that of his enemies or his rivals in arms.   None,
perhaps, are more ready to admit his talent than the
soldiers of the Northern army— the admission, perhaps,
you may say, is but politic, as adding to the credit
due to his defeat, whenever that may be effected—
but, at any rate, the Northern soldiers are candid
enough to confess, what their journalists with asinine
obstinacy deny, that they have not a general who can
hold a candle to him.

But there were plenty of other passengers besides
the soldiers, all affable and communicative ; and from
them we gathered, in the course of conversation, an in-
definite number of diametrically opposite views of the
coming political contest.   We had Republicans,
Democrats, Copper-heads, and Abolitionists on board,
and each representative of every one of these parties
held different ideas about everything from those which
his fellow-representatives entertained.   The subject of
greatest difference was the war itself in its political
aspect.   Politics, of course, every one in America talks.
It comes more naturally to them than their A B C.
They seem to suck it in with their mother's milk, for
the women are " bluer " in politics than the men ;
they lisp it in the nursery, babble it in the schoolroom, fight about it in the academy, and drink over it in
the bars, till the whole nation becomes saturated with

the virus of what I may call " politicomanie," a disease which injects its poisonous infusions into every member of the state with such fatal effect, that the free working of the whole body is incalculably cramped and crippled by it. No department is free from its influence. Courts of Justice are victims to its sway. Judges and juries cannot resist the party feeling which its constant presence everywhere engenders. Stump oratory and platform declamation feed it. Paltry pulpiteers propagate it, and hot-headed journalists subsist upon it. You hear it in every walk of life, read it in every printed page of paper. In the cars, on the boats, in the streets, at the hotels, in the churches, nothing but politics. Soldiers, sailors, tinkers, tailors, parsons, ploughboys, porters, waiters, know no subject of conversation but the eternal politics. You think, in your innocence, to avoid it in the drawing-room, but you find the ladies as keen upon it as the men. Elderly ladies of the Republican persuasion lecture you upon the crimes of the Democratic leaders. Youthful beauties, that would do honour to an English ball room, question you upon the doctrine of State rights. Middle-aged females bore you to death with puzzling interrogations about your own Constitution. And if in disgust you retire to your bedroom, and happen to ring for the chambermaid, she asks you whether you think the Democrats will withdraw the

fourth plank of their platform, and if they do what
will be the consequence.

Well, then, you will not wonder that the chief subject of conversation was politics, nor, perhaps, will you
be surprised to hear that, by the time our passage up the
Mississippi came to an end, I had had a great deal more
of politics than was good for either me or my temper.
We discussed them with the captain (a very seedy
gentleman, by the bye), with the steward (a seedier
one), with the engineers, the soldiers, the gentlemen
passengers, and the lady passengers; and such a
muddle-headed maze of mystification did my brain get
lost in, after three days' incessant struggling to deduce
some consistent result from the thousand-and-one ideas
with which it was assailed, that I shall, out of chari-
table feelings for yours, abstain from inflicting upon
you what, I feel sure, will do you no good. I will only
add that the chief cause of my mystification was a
smart, affable young lady, who laid down her theories
of the science in such an authoritative style of diction,
that I was at first completely awed into the mildest
submission to her precepts. But her father, in com-
passion, I presume, for the evident weakness of my
defensive armour, rebuked her with an admonition to
hit somebody of her own size, and she spared me
accordingly. I saw a good deal of this party during
our passage. They were extremely agreeable people.
The father had just come from Chicago, whither he

had been sent as a delegate to the great Democratic
Convention.   He lived in the State of New York,
where I have no doubt he was a man of some influence
amongst the extreme Democrats, for he was a copper-
head, every inch of him, and, accordingly, all his
talents, time, and toil were devoted exclusively to
thwarting the Government in the conduct of the war,
and promoting the interests of the enemy.   He spoke
despondingly of his country as the worst-governed on
the face of the inhabited globe, heaped upon Old Abe
such a mountain of abuse as only an American would
condescend to pitch upon him, snarled at the ministers,
jeered at the generals, and ridiculed the troops.   It
was all done too in a gentlemanly way, for he was a
man of good education and refined manner; but I
must say I have no sympathy with those whose patriotism, like Mr. Bright's, requires a Ross's telescope to
be seen at all—a very "milk and watery way"—consisting solely in a love of their country's protection without a thought for the protection of their country.   In
fact I have a great contempt for copperheads in general; they are simply Confederates who have not the
pluck to avow it.

   The affable young lady and her papa and mamma and
brother engaged me in conversation till late in the
evening, when it struck me that the scenery through
which we were passing was worth observance—and I
looked out and found it to be so.   We had passed, in the

afternoon, through a vast sheet of water, five miles
wide and many long, where the river expands into a
lake or broad, which bears the name of Lake Pepin ;
thence past Wanona's Rock, the crag whence the
Indian maiden flung herself in despair at the persecu-
tions wreaked on her by her tribe for her wilful love
of the paleface; past the Chimney Mountain, a romantic formation on the left bank ; and Redwing, a prettily
situated town, which the parting rays of the sinking
sun lit up, as we stopped there for the mails, with
such an array of red and gold as neither pen nor
pencil could depict. The river's breadth was much
less here, and under the tumbled forms of the rocky
bluffs, which girt the water's edge, we lay for a time
to take in fuel, and glad enough to rest there, for the
scene was exquisite. Then on again to the West, into
the golden glow that streamed down to us over the
flood, and as we went the gold and the blue above us
faded into a soft hazy green, and darkness set in at
once without a twilight.

It was eleven at night when I was roused from my
reveries by the announcement that we had met the
other steamer into which we were to be transferred, a
boat of lighter draught than that on which we then
were, and better adapted for navigating the shallows
which, of course, became more numerous as we
ascended the river. The two boats came to an anchor
in the middle of the stream, and a flat-bottomed barge

10

with a plank thrown across to it from each boat
served to establish a communication between them. In
a minute an illumination was extemporised on board
each of the boats by means of a lighted brazier, filled
with tar and such like combustibles, and beneath the
lurid glare shed by the blazing matter ensued such a
scene of noise and bustle as I never shall forget.
What a subject for a picture that would have been!
The bustling and confusion amongst the two sets of
passengers changing from boat to boat, the awkward
meetings on the narrow planks, the flights of the boxes
and carpet-bags pell-mell into the bottom of the barge,
the hurry and scurry amongst the black stewards, the
falling embers from the burning braziers, the life and
light in the centre of the stream, the blackness and
solitude all around.   With all the confusion, however,
the change of cargoes was an affair of but a few
minutes ; but the scene was so strange, so novel, the
fiery redness of the braziers, and the objects illuminated by them so unearthly, that I see it all as vividly
now as if it were still before me, and often, I dare say,
shall I call up in my dreams this midnight boat-chang-
ing on the Mississippi.

The new vessel, a minature of the other, was much
more stuffy, close, and uncomfortable. Berths of
course were out of the question. Sleeping room on
the floors was at a premium ; and mattresses unobtain-
able, for love or money.   But fraud got me a quarter

of one, and on my allotted portion of it I somehow or
other contrived to doze in the midst of a perfect maze
of arms, and legs, and heads, and feet, interspersed
with hats, coats, collars, ties, and boots; the oddest
medley that I ever saw upon the floor of any room;
and, judging from her convulsive laughter at my
appearance or rather dis-appearance in the midst of it,
so too thought the affable young lady. I was very
tired, however, and did not heed her playful sallies,
but my slumbers were not healthy or refreshing by
any means, and when the black steward at 4.30 a.m.
tipped up the mattresses to clear and sweep the room, I
was quite content to get away from the atmosphere,
and the fleas.

You may wonder possibly how they managed to
cook us any meals, seeing that their space was so
limited. I know I did, and so I do now. I can offer
no explanation. I am sure there was no kitchen, and
I know there was no fire. I never saw any cook on
board, nor anything cooking. But you may stake
your fortune, that where there are any Americans,
there will always be plenty to eat (and generally I
should say the converse holds good, and that where
there is plenty to eat there will always be Americans),
and therefore I felt perfectly confident that our appetites would be well cared for, and so they were. We
had hot meats on the table for breakfast, dinner, tea,
and supper; but I am to this day as ignorant as the

astonished parent in Beauty and the Beast how or whence they got there.

The next day was much like the preceding; ditto the scenery—only that the river banks drew nearer together, which I thought added considerably to the beauty of the stream. The only variation in the day's proceedings was some remarkably bad rifle practice by the soldiers at the numerous herons upon the sand banks, and a still more indifferent practice at larger objects in the shape of cows in the adjacent meadows. Nothing astonishes me more than the reckless use of firearms in this country. Men and boys play with "six-shooters" as if they were as harmless as children's pop-guns. The beautiful science of the P. R. ("Prize Ring" fair reader) is utterly scouted in the States for the more effective satisfaction administered by the revolver. The natural arm of an American, offensive or defensive, is not—pardon the "bull" —his fist, but his pistol. He carries it about with him in its leathern receptacle beneath his coat, at all times, and in all places. He knows nothing of the European etiquette which restricts its use to the hour of cock-crow, and regards the orthodox accompaniment of coffee as a superlative absurdity. Young or old, high or low, he must have his six-shooter. The father and brothers of the affable young lady, refined and well educated as they were, carried their pistols as a matter of course. True, when I expostulated with them, they excused themselves by saying that they were intended only as a means of defence against the possible assaults of the soldiers; but the copperheads delight in making martyrs of themselves, or rather holding themselves out as victims to a martyrdom which is purely imaginary, and I consider the pretext of these two gentlemen nothing but a specious defence of a barbarous usage which must condemn itself in the eyes of any educated man. However that may be, there is the established habit, and if civilians are habitually so reckless in the employment of murderous weapons, it was not to be marvelled at that the soldiers, tolerably inured to the atrocities of the guerilla warfare of the West, should exhibit a pre-eminent heedlessness in the promiscuous use of their rifles. They spent the whole morning in random shots at everything live or dead that offered a convenient mark. They seemed to have a perfectly unlimited supply of the U. S. ammunition, and being citizens of a free republic, were free to do what they liked with it,—an elysian perfection of unconditional license in the boasted possession of which a Yankee is for ever impressing upon you the superiority of his political condition, and which, in Yankee parlance, consists in the right of every man to do as he "dam pleases." I never saw any people more alive to the existence of their constitutional rights than the soldiers in the present instance. How many hundred

shots were fired I know not, nor do I see why I or
anybody else on board was not shot every bit as much
as the objects actually aimed at.   If I saw one rifle
pointed at my head, I saw a hundred.   Revolvers
were swung carelessly about with much less caution
than is exhibited in an English cover.   Across the
deck, through the rigging, out of the saloon-windows,
over the hats of the passengers, anyhow, was kept up
an irregular discharge of the most independent firing
I have ever witnessed.   Nobody seemed to mind it,
ladies and children took little or no notice of it, and,
stranger still, no harm seemed to come of it, either to
those on board or the objects of assault.   I thought I
saw a poor cow struck, but to the disappointment of
her enemy she walked off untouched.

Soon after mid-day we landed at a point in the river
beyond which the shallows would not admit our boat.
There we were to wait for a still lighter tug to carry
us up to St. Paul's.   I was tired of the river, and
hearing that the city was only twelve miles off proposed a walk.   It was accepted by about twenty of
the passengers, which, considering that an American
never walks, could only be accounted for by their being
as weary of the boat as myself; and under the guidance of one who said he knew the road, our party
accordingly started.   The path lay at first up through a
thin belt of elm, oak, and beech—pretty enough in
itself, but too little—and thence out across ten miles

of the hottest, dustiest plain I ever traversed. It was a real joy to see the distant roofs and steeples of St. Paul's in view as we came down again to the river, and better still to be upon the curious bridge which connects the low level bank, on which we then were with the high chalky bluff on which the city stands—a most distressingly untraditional bridge, all on the oblique and very awkward, like a great clumsy fire-escape propped up against a high wall—but best of all to be splashing about, and rinsing off the very palpable results of a three days' roughing it on those awful boats, down in the cool depths of a glorious bath, beneath the shelter of what the Paulites call their " Internay-tional Hoe-tel."

VIII.

FROM THE MISSISSIPPI TO THE ST. LAWRENCE.

WASHINGTON;
October 10th.

St. Paul's is as yet in its infancy. But a very few years ago this precocious child of the prairie was not even thought of, and now she has not only assumed to herself the name of a city—every American town does that, whether it has any right to the appellation or no—but she has summoned together, while hardly into her teens, a population of twenty thousand inhabitants, and, when fairly of age, will rival in size many a European capital. At present her prosperity seems to be due to the fur trade, which is enormous. Every other shop is a furrier's. The streets are redolent of hides. Wolf, fox, bear, mink, wild-cat— every specimen of the genus " vermin "—is to be seen dangling in the windows. And, strange to say, even in the headquarters of the furriers there is carried on such a system of deception as I should have thought incredible, had I not seen it actually at work. Chicanery, I suppose, like charity, begins at home; and so in the heart of the great fur country commences an elaborate process of dyeing, and staining, and veneering, which would astonish the belles of London and Paris, who flatter themselves that they pay for the genuine article. I do not believe one muff in a hundred is what it purports to be. Sable is concocted out of anything, mink is cooked up out of the mangiest of mangy skins. Ermine is deliberately painted on the seediest of repulsive hides. The manufacture of ancient coins, Yankee shoddy, Lillo pickles, or London milk, could not reveal greater scholarship in the art of humbug. I wonder what proportion of the cloaks, muffs, boas and tippets, that I see in London does really come off the backs of animals whose name they bear, seeing that the genuine thing is so extremely rare in the district of its native home. But the wreck of the Royal George has proved large enough to furnish a city of English mansions, the *santo sudario* or sacred winding-sheet of Turin has produced sufficient stuff to furnish sails for the fleets of Italy, the bullets picked up on the field of Waterloo would have slaughtered the whole population of Europe, and why should not the sables and minks of St. Paul's be numerous enough to satisfy the demands of all the toilettes of the civilised world?

But "fur" is not the only staff of life to the

inhabitants of St. Paul's.   Agriculture increases its area, and every day sees new settlers arriving and fresh lands subjected to the plough.   Commerce follows in its wake, and being on the highway of the Mississippi, the great artery of the North West, the city must rise in importance with the development of the country, and the signs of its future rise are already visible.   In itself it is by no means beautiful. It stands favorably on a chalky eminence above the river, and from a terrace upon the cliff there is an extensive view of the surrounding country; but there are no fine houses, as in Chicago, nor handsome streets and towering warehouses.   The buildings are irregular and low, and almost as mean as in the western end of Oxford Street.   I do not know that I can say anything of them more derogatory to their character than that.

The sun next day was equatorial.   I am not quite sure that I know what that may be, but I know that the thermometer in the shade was up to 100°, and standing in the sun was an absolute impossibility. They say that nothing is ever seen in the daytime in the streets of Malta but Englishmen and dogs, and certainly there was nothing else that day in the streets of St. Paul's.   But, protected as we were with umbrellas, and tolerably inured to noonday roastings, we were totally unable to stand the blaze and glare. Less than five minutes in the open air (to be properly delicate) dissolved me utterly into floods of tears, and five minutes more, as I retreated home again, fried me dry and stupid.

But time was precious, and there was plenty to be seen in the neighbourhood; so, after a brief siesta, we determined to stand for neither sun nor ceremony, and, divesting ourselves of coat and waistcoat, took our seats in an open calèche and started out for a drive into the country. The afternoon was slightly cooler, but still uncomfortably hot; how the horses pulled under it I cannot imagine, but they travelled well, and we were soon eight miles from St. Paul's, crossing the Mississippi in a ferry-boat beneath the frowning heights of Fort Snelling. The ferry-boat was worked in the same way as those upon the Rhine, by the means of a rope and running wheel upon it, the boat being laid obliquely across the stream and left to the current to force it along the rope. A steep climb up the other bank landed us at the gate of the fort. It was a very shady specimen of a fortification, having no pretensions whatever to engineering skill, and less to comfort and accommodation. The only attraction it possessed in our eyes was the fact that it then contained some Indian prisoners lately captured in the frontier war, whom we were anxious to inspect. We stated our wish to the sentinel, which was peremptorily refused; but our driver, a capital fellow, was as anxious as ourselves that we should miss none of the lions of

the country, and, hastily dismounting, tackled the
bewildered sentry with such an ebullition of remon-
strative volubility—the pith of which appeared to be
that the colonel was a great friend of his and would
let him in directly if he only knew he was there—that
the sentry yielded in despair, and handed us to a
corporal to be duly lionised round.

We were shown into a good-sized airy chamber, and
there, at the further end, chained by the leg to a
ring in the wall, sat the objects of our search, the two
Indian prisoners.   They were both princes of their
tribe, very fine specimens of their race, the Sioux,
large limbed, well proportioned, lithe and supple as
tigers.   One, who rejoiced in the name of " Little
Six," was of great age, more than ninety, but he
seemed to lack none of his youthful vigour, and saving
a few gray hairs upon his head, time had laid no
finger-mark upon him.   The other, "Medicine Bottle,"
was of middle age, of handsome cast of countenance,
and splendid frame.   He had lately been adorning
himself in his war paint—which they both delighted
in daubing on and washing off again two or three
times a week—and had, in a fit of eccentricity, removed
the whole of it except a bright vermilion streak down
the middle of his hair, which parted in the centre of
his forehead.   They were both engaged in eating nuts,
brought in by their friends in the neighbourhood, who
seemed to be permitted access to them much more

readily than I should have supposed expedient; and in this operation they slacked not for a moment all the time we were inspecting and making our remarks upon them, simply lingering in the mastication of every other nut to cool themselves with a fan that lay beside each; for they seemed to suffer from the heat as much and more than we did, though their dress was of the most unscrupulously meagre kind. They looked harmless enough as we saw them, and it was difficult to trace any evidence in their features of the ferocity which had characterised their recent deeds. And yet they had both taken the lead in one of the most barbarous massacres of whites that had occurred for years. Little Six was in the habit of boasting that he had on that occasion successfully scalped thirteen women and children, and as many men. What Medicine Bottle's particular feats had been we did not hear. They were both under sentence of execution, of course, but that did not seem to trouble them. I suppose they consoled themselves with the hope that they were going to the Good Spirit, into whose presence the scalping of whites is, I believe, the surest passport.

I have often wondered at the almost paradoxical effect upon the aboriginal heathen races of contact with Christianity. I never have been able to understand how it is that the religion of the Cross, as it sheds its warm light in the presence of the native mind, seems to call into life and action all the evil seeds that rankle there, and, once vivified and brought to the surface, choke both soul and body. Whence is this mysterious anomaly? I have asked a great many questions here with a view to get some clue to the secret of the notorious extermination that has been stealthily but steadily, like a hidden cancer, doing its deadly work upon the North American Indians, from the day that Columbus first set foot upon the soil. Well-informed people with whom I have conversed have their different theories, but no one of them appears to me satisfactory. Philosophers propound it as an established axiom, without a thought of the horrors of the principle it involves, that all aboriginal races are, by that very fact, doomed to speedy and inevitable destruction as soon as they come in contact with people of European origin. They declare it to be only a question of time, and call it idle to admit any other basis of calculation when dealing with this matter in a practical way. And, sad to say, modern experience points to the truth of the philosophers' view. Notwithstanding the well-meant efforts of philanthropists to preserve and civilise the scattered remnants of the human family which the progress of enterprise brings to knowledge, sooner or later the same fate overtakes all savage races. Do what governments will to preserve the inferior race from the aggression of the superior, the natives " die in the white man's breath ;" and contact with Christianity, which should, at least, confer a more extended knowledge of physics, if not a higher moral standard, seems to be to the aboriginal tribes the sure signal of present extinction. Various causes may be assigned which play their part in this wholesale murder. The importation of European diseases, particularly smallpox, a scourge which commits amongst the savage races such devastation as the plague-days of old London could not match for virulence—the introduction of "fire-water" and tobacco, to which they evince an unconquerable propensity—and the infusion of an unhealthy taste for all the worst practices of civilised communities—are powerful agencies in the dark work of destruction. Border warfare with the new comers and suicidal contests amongst themselves reduce their numbers, perhaps, more surely than the insidious agencies of civilised vice. But cruelty of borderers and international strife will not alone account for the prodigious revelations of statistics. What there is in the savage nature so abhorrent from the "white" that the two will not mingle, but must contend in antagonistic rivalry till the weaker is absorbed in the more powerful solvent, has never been explained. Various efforts are being made to induce the two opposite characters to assimilate themselves, but without avail. The Indians in Canada and the Northern States, who have their own allotted territory, cannot even be persuaded by the example of the active industry around them to till the soil which the respective

governments reserve to them.   They are content to
inhabit a desert in the centre of a garden—to typify
death in the midst of life.   The phenomenon of the
disease is still a mystery, and no treatment yet attempted can resuscitate the fast-failing patient.

Behind the fort was a large camp containing several
thousand men, recruits, chiefly from the North Western
districts.   Their tents were mathematically set out—
large, neat, and orderly.   On the training-ground beside
them the men were being put through their manual
exercise.   The exhibition was by no means perfect, but
the performers were fresh hands, and the veterans who
were instructing them did not seem to know much
about it.   They were to march shortly against the
Indians.

From the terrace on which the fort stands there is a
fine view of the Mississippi, and the Minnesota, which
falls into it at this point.   We gazed at it for a short
time, and then drove on to the falls of Minne-ha-ha,
immortalised by Longfellow.   I did not expect to
come upon such a scene as the poet has idealised, nor
an encampment of Indians on the margin of the
stream such as he has pictured, which, however it
might have added to the landscape, would in their
present white-blood-thirstiness have much disconcerted
our party; but I own I was not a little disappointed
to find that the Falls of Minne-ha-ha were now little
else than a tea-garden.   Some enterprising speculator

from the East has located himself on the roadside, and there has run up a small inn for the sale of spirituous liquors, and seems to find the custom of the numerous pilgrims to the scene pay him for his trouble. I thought that we should be the only visitors; in fact, I did not imagine that in this out of the way corner of the world there could be any extensive number of excursionists to a spot so retired from town or village. But an assertion of an intention on my part to bathe at the bottom of his garden made him very red and angry, and no assurance that I had not the smallest idea he had any visitors, or the slightest desire to insult them, nothing, in fact, but the purchase of "a drink" pacified his indignation.

The immediate vicinity of the Falls is one of the prettiest little glens conceivable; very narrow, very deep, charmingly wooded, and altogether lovely; at the head of it is a bold rock, and from the top of the rock *should* fall the cascade which we had come to see. But, alas, the thirsty sun, which had so sadly reduced the Mississippi, had unmercifully sucked out the vitals of the poor little stream, and instead of bubbling and frothing over the precipice in the sparkling, joyous fulness of heart which has given it its name of the "laughing waters", it was then all shrivelled and parched, and could only drop a few silent tears of melancholy for its wasted condition. I really felt quite sad for the little rivulet, though inclined to

11

doubt whether it ever deserved the eulogies which poets and painters have bestowed upon it; but there certainly was the sweetest little pool at the base of the rock, so dark, and deep, and still, that I almost forgave the stream for the disappointment it caused me at looking so insignificant.

We did not stay loug—*pace* poet and painter—but drove on to Minneapolis, a very pretty town on the right bank of the Mississippi, and thence across by a suspension bridge to St. Anthony on the left bank, a similar town, and there we halted for a short time to get a peep at the Falls of St. Anthony. But the water was too low, and all that was to be seen was a mass of tumbled rock of every size and shape, with here and there a little eddy in the gaps between the crags, indications of the terrible rapids that break and foam about them when the river is at its proper height. Thence we mounted the steep which leads to the summit of the bank, and so along the edge of the cliff, till the sun went down upon one of the prettiest scenes I have met with on this Continent. The river ran beneath us at the bottom of a narrow gorge, its banks wooded to the water's edge, and dotted with an occasional house that peeped forth from the dense dark foliage; and behind us, as we looked back, lay the broken rocks of the Falls, with the towers and steeples of St. Anthony, and the bridge and Minneapolis beyond. The sunlight hues were fairy-like, bright and diversified as those which I had seen on the Mississippi ; and if anything rewarded me for the long weary journey I had taken to get to this, the farthest point of my North-Western excursion, it was this evening's drive.

Darkness soon set in, and we turned away from the river to make straight for home. The road was primitive and exciting, for it was traversed by numerous gullies, which were spanned by wooden bridges composed simply of a lot of loose planks, very uneven, and very rotten. Some of the planks were broken half off, some had great apertures in their centre, some had gone altogether. Why the horses were not thrown or killed, or why the carriage was not let through or upset, to this day I cannot satisfactorily answer. Our driver said the animals were used to the bridges, and so they seemed, for if they did get any one or more of their legs through the timbers, they did not appear to be the least disconcerted, but struggled methodically till they got them out, and resumed their course. At one chasm they took a fair leap, and the carriage followed them across it in splendid style. I think from my experience of this drive, that cross-country carriage practice would be much less difficult than you might imagine; and I should suggest to our Irish Turfites a steeple chase in chariots, as an extremely practicable, and I would venture to think sufficiently "sensational" termination of a day's sport.

A little incident occurred on the road eminently
illustrative of the relative positions of master and servant in the model republic. Some time after leaving
the river we came to a small roadside inn, at which
our driver pulled up to water his horses. This done,
he called to us in the carriage—

"Now then gentlemen, come on, guess we'd better
have a drink; it's 'nation hot, and I feel a mind to
throw myself outside a glass of something. What
shall it be?"

I thought it was a Yankee's cool way of putting to
us the invariable suggestion of every English cabman
with whom you are unlucky enough to fraternise, that
"you *might* stand him something" (which something,
by-the-bye, I have always found to be gin and water)
and though a little taken aback by the apparent cool-
ness of the demand, I felt myself the need of a little
something, and acquiesced.

The something was duly ordered and demolished,
no matter what it was; and before leaving the counter
I pulled out and offered to the spiritual medium behind it sufficient paper to defray the aggregate cost of
the party's drinks. I never made a more unfortunate
mistake. My cousin, more *au fait* in the etiquette of
this continent, knew the meaning of the driver's invi-
tation, and smiled at my innocence; but how was any
one who had experience of the exhaustive and expensive capacities of the British working man's throat, to

divine that this driver was about to treat his fare himself? Imagine the satisfaction I shall have on my return home in explaining to the first cabman who insinuates that "It's wery cold, sir," if it does not rain, or "Wery wet, sir," if it does, in that thick and beery tone which is universally accepted as the British equivalent of the less scrupulous continental demand for *pour boire* or *trinkgeld*—imagine, I say, the pleasure of representing to such an one how the tables are turned here, and how grand a thing it would be if our working classes had a little of that independence and self-respect which forbids the American to demand, over and above his due wages, those extortional fees which in Europe must almost necessarily be paid to secure ordinary civility. It is one of the greatest charms, perhaps, of travelling in this country that fees are incidents of an advanced state of society at present here unknown. It would be almost as strange to a Yankee to be asked by a porter for a "tip," as it would be to an Englishman to get that individual to do anything without one. It seems such a perfect Utopia of hotel life to be allowed to quit the establishment without "remembering" the boots, that I find great difficulty in keeping my hand from wandering to my pocket when I take my leave of that worthy at the door. But I make the most of the improved system, which saves the traveller so much small change, for I shall not get the benefit of it much

longer. The New Yorkers, I understand, are progres-
sively advancing into the mal-practices of the more
perfect civilisation of the old world, and I know very
well that the first thing I shall have to do on landing
in England will be to "tip" somebody.

I do not think I have anything further to say about
St. Paul's. My cousin and I considered that we had
nothing more to see there, so the next morning we
put ourselves on board the wretched little boat which
had brought the up passengers the last twelve miles of
their voyage from the South, and started back for
Canada. I have no need to describe the down journey
on the Mississippi. It was an exact repetition of our
upward trip; the same tiresome change of boats, only
this time reversed, each fresh boat being a size larger
than the last, though the benefit of the change was
always counterbalanced by an unaccountable elasticity
in the persons of the passengers, which filled and
crowded the largest of our boats to all intents and
purposes as much as the smallest; the same monotony
of scenery; the same kind of *compagnons de voyage*
(barring the affable young lady, whom I missed sadly);
the same conversations with the soldiers, this time *en
route* for the scene of war, and not very well pleased
about it; the same dreary railroad journey from La
Cross, but in a more uncomfortable car, only that we
left the main line 100 miles short of Chicago, and

" slanted off " to the great city of Milwaukee on Lake Michigan.

There is nothing in Milwaukee but what may be found in every other American city that I have seen, and I believe in all that I have not seen. Long straight handsome streets, wide boulevards, enormous hotels, colossal warehouses, gigantic stores, spacious wharves, and cyclopean " elevators " ; a large imposing post-office, three or four passable churches, advertisements upon any vacant surface, a railway station in the middle of the high street, tracks for street cars everywhere, good paving nowhere ; crowds in the stores, at the entrances to the hotels, in the street cars, and round the offices of the local journals ; buggies rushing in all directions, always apparently late for a train, like the butchers' carts in London ; abundance of colour, plenty of noise, tobacco-smoke, heat, and dust.

We stayed but a few hours in Milwaukee, and got on board a steamer to cross the lake to Grand Haven. It was a rough night, and made me feel squeamish, but I got to sleep and woke up in the harbour on the opposite side. Then the cars again all next day and all the next night, through the great state of Michigan, of which I shall say nothing, because what I saw of it exactly resembled what I have already attempted to describe of the Western States, and so to Detroit, on the border of the American territory.

Detroit was exactly like Milwaukee, only larger and much older, and, being a wet day, it was dirty and abominable. We glanced hastily at the city, and after careful scrutiny by the U.S. pickets at the wharf, who seemed half inclined to stop us as deserters or Confederate spies, were off again across Lake St. Clair, in the most uncomfortably crowded steamer (where in the world were all the people going?) to Windsor, the border town of the Canadian territory, smaller than Detroit and dirtier, and thence a hundred miles up the Great Western line to ——— London. It was past midnight when we reached the hotel, and you may imagine, or rather, perhaps, you cannot imagine, how tired we were after this tremendous stretch of cars and steam-boats. But we were well "fixed up" in the way of beds, a luxury which we had not enjoyed for five nights (for we had last tucked ourselves up at St. Paul's), and we both slept like children.

London is a miniature of its namesake in the old country. Its inhabitants, I have no doubt, flatter themselves that the likeness is sufficiently correct to justify their assumption of the title, and as far as names go (if there is anything in a name) the resemblance is perfect. There is an Oxford Street, a Regent Street, a Holborn (with an "H"), a Bond Street, Piccadilly, and Pall Mall; there is a Thames, too, very different though from its mud-running progenitor of Westminster— a clear, lively little stream, with high sloping banks and rocky bed. But it is all on such a diminutive scale that the comparison is ludicrous. It is like taking a sight at the British Metropolis through the wrong end of a telescope. Everything is so absurdly dwarfed, that I could scarce restrain my laughter at the toy-like imitation. But it is like enough to the original to remind me forcibly of many of its characteristics. It was wet and muddy and extremely dirty; it was foggy, too (though not yellow); there was plenty of bustle and excitement in the streets, for the sessions were on; and the houses were low and irregular. But on the whole I did not find that I was so impressed as I ought to have been by these touching mementoes of my native city. Of course I kept to myself my own ideas as to the success of the imitation, and if the Canadian Londoners fondly imagine that their little village is worthy to bear the name of its prototype, by all means let them enjoy the innocent delusion. It pleases them, and it does not hurt us.

One word, however, I must have with these Londoners before I take leave of them. I do not know whether I have said anything about the atrocious system of advertisements (pronounce third syllable long like " size "), which on this continent is carried to a preposterous extravagance, but the principle is so characteristic of the people, that, at the risk of re-petition, I must enlarge upon it. Any one who has read the great Barnum's life will recollect the efficacy of his famous advertisements about his elephant and his museum, and how he bought up for several consecutive days the whole of one of the most influential journals of New York, for the purpose of filling every one of its columns with a simple but expressive statement that "The elephant had arrived." The example of the great professor in the art of humbug has been to a certain extent followed at home, where our 'Daily Telegraph' may have been seen for months together lending itself to the remarkably interesting announcement down the full length of one of its columns, that Messrs. Samuel are brothers and tailors. You might fancy, perhaps, that the English had advanced to a sufficiently perfect comprehension of the science. But I assure you that by the side of the American and Canadian professors of the art, we are uncommonly "small potatoes." What do you think of a barrister informing you by a notice at the foot of a dinner *carte* that he undertakes cases on easy terms, and is ready to be consulted at all hours? In justice to the profession I think I ought to say that I saw this at Ottawa. What do you think of a parson notifying the public by a daub of red letters upon the edge of the curb-stone that he will administer the sacrament on Sunday next, and hopes his friends will attend? In justice to his profession I think I ought to add that I saw this at Milwaukee.

The advertisements in the journals are as singular

and instructive, much more spicy than our English institutions, and far more unscrupulous and indelicate. Play-bills, lecture-bills, and placards of all sorts attain a far higher perfection in the New World than in the Old. Here is a specimen of one which I read in the entrance hall of my hotel in Chicago. I consider it the *beau ideal* of advertising ingenuity:

To-morrow,
at **SIX** o'clock,
Professor Benson
will give a performance
in the art of legerdemain,
to which **LADIES** & gentlemen
are invited to come as
early as they please.
The Professor
will be
FOUND
at the New Theatre, Pine St.,
whither he has lately come from
New York.
He will not exactly
raise the **DEAD** to life,
but will perform feats only second
to that in mystery of execution
IN A
way that will fully
satisfy the expectations
of all who may honour him with
a visit.
BOX
office open from 10 to 4 p.m.

There were plenty besides which amused me about as much. I do not think I have seen any of those long strings of "boardmen," that may at any time be observed winding serpent-like down our narrow streets, in mute, inglorious silence, defiant of peeler and pedestrian. But if there are no boards on the backs of the men, there are plenty on the fronts of the houses, and some of the finest streets in the cities which I have visited are totally disfigured with unsightly placards that utterly destroy the symmetry of the architecture. London, I think, surpassed all these cities in the wanton profusion of its boards and placards. Its Regent Street looked much more like the grand alley of a country fair than the high thoroughfare of a respectable city. The buildings were covered from base to roof with staring advertisements of their contents. Their owner's names were blazoned about in the largest type and the gaudiest colours. Across the pavement, on either side, at every ten feet's interval, protruded huge transverse boards, proclaiming to the visitors the style and trade of their respective masters; and often as not, above the boards, high up in the centre of the houses, was fixed a colossal representative of the articles sold below. A boot, perhaps, that would have matched the ten-leagued Wellingtons of the legendary giants; a hat that would have covered the whole Blue-coat school; a tea-pot capacious enough for an evening fight at the editor of the Re-

cord's; a chair big enough for Banting; a joint of
meat which could only have been cut from a megathe-
rium; a stiff ghost-like pair of unmentionables, striding
half way across the street, into which the Colossus of
Rhodes could have stepped with ease; and gig umbrellas, as in Tottenham Court Road, Gamp-like and
innumerable. Then there was another curious feature
in the advertisement disease, which I had frequently
remarked before, and that was the presence in
front of every shoemaker's shop of a gigantic model
boot, always much larger than the one suspended
from the house above, and always bright vermilion. I recollect first noticing these preposterous
objects in the humble village of Ottawa, and laughing
immoderately at the monstrosity. They go on wheels,
and every evening at shop-closing time are wheeled
into bed for the night by the united efforts of the
master boot-maker and his underlings. I hardly expected to meet with such a practical illustration of the
famous picture of Gulliver's boot in the hands of the
natives of Lilliput. Such are the ungainly forms and
grotesque erections with which the people of this continent delight to disfigure their handsome streets. The
vice is by no means unknown with us at home, but it
has reached in the New World a pitch of unlicensed
vulgarity which it is a crying disgrace to the civic authorities not to suppress or check.

I have already said something about the agricultural

districts of the Western States, and now that I am
speaking of a journey through the most fertile of the
rich soils of Upper Canada, I hardly like to refrain
from adding my small tribute of praise to the profusion of munificence with which Nature has showered
down her golden gifts upon the land. The earth teems
with productive energy, and I could tell you many
stories I have heard of its marvellous fertility; but I
have palmed off upon you enough of what I have only
picked up second-hand. Still there is one remark I
must make, and that is, that, so far as I can learn, all
this wonderful natural wealth cannot compete for settlers
with those of the Western prairies. Now Canada, it
seems, has been trying to work what appears to me an
impolitic system, whereby she has added a few thousand
dollars to her revenue at the cost of a double number
of immigrants. For every dollar of purchase money
she screws out of one poor settler, she loses at least
a couple of other settlers. And immigration is her
very life. The increase of her population is the increase of her exports, her commerce, her means of
self-preservation, her rank in the catalogue of nations.
But yet it seems to be an admitted fact that all her
efforts are of little avail to turn the current of
European emigration into channels of her own. Far,
far the larger portion of each ship's cargo that reaches
this continent eventually finds a resting-place in the
Western States. The Americans, thoroughly awake

to the important use to which their unappropriated
lands might be applied, have for years past adopted
the policy of giving them away to actual settlers
without charge or condition, save a certain term's re-
sident occupation and a fixed amount of annual tillage.
Why should not Canada do the same? Why exact a
petty price from those who come to hew out for themselves and their children a home in the wild forest,
and give the sweat of their brow to the service of
their adopted country? Surely there is more to be
gained by the industry of a hardy settler upon a hundred acres than the contemptible hundred dollars
squeezed out of him as its price. Upper Canada has,
I believe, three millions of surveyed lands parcelled
out into fixed townships, and ready for any who choose
to take them; and these would provide farms for
thirty thousand families. She ought to have every
advantage over her neighbours just now—peace, prosperity, surplus revenue, good government, good laws;
and yet she drives men to forego all these for the sake
of a paltry sum, which at first starting they can ill
spare; and while she continues this short-sighted
policy the Western States will outbid her.

We left London the next morning, and by dinner-
time were in Toronto, and not sorry to get a little
quiet after our hurried and continuous journey from
the West. The fatigues of the trip were a little too
much for me, and sent me to bed with a sharp attack

of bilious fever; but my cousin and his wife took great care of me, and after a week's rest I was able to proceed with them to Cornwall on the St. Lawrence, to stay with the Hon. J. Sandfield Macdonald, the late Premier of the Canadian Parliament. I had a very pleasant visit in his house, and recruited my health satisfactorily in the more bracing air of that climate. He and his daughters were extremely attentive, and it was with much regret that I said good-bye after five days under his hospitable roof. Mr. Macdonald himself, or Sandfield, as he is generally called, to distinguish him from the numerous Scots of his name who have settled in and colonised the neighbourhood of Cornwall, has had for many years the most extensive practice at the Canadian bar, but since entering on official life has left it principally to his partner; and now that he is out of office he devotes the greater part of his time to a couple of farms, that he is bringing into a high state of cultivation by drainage and such-like improvements, which appear to be novelties to the inhabitants. His house is open at all hours to all who choose to avail themselves of the privilege; two extra places are laid at dinner for casual visitors, and nothing pleases the host so much as to see these casually filled.

The assizes were on at the time I was with him, and the judges on circuit dined at his table, so that I had a grand opportunity of seeing the *élite* of the legal profession. I was not much impressed with their general appearance or display of talent, except in the case of the chancellor—for he, you must know, goes circuit too. As to dignity of look and language, I saw very little of that. The conversation was so free and easy, the bottle so locomotive, that stiffness and formality had no more place there than in a college common room. The ex-premier was jovial as a schoolboy, brimful of anecdotes and humour. The chancellor capped his racy stories with stories of his own still racier; and the evening closed with a performance by the host, on a very bad fiddle, of a series of Scotch reels, to the accompaniment of the piano. The next morning, where should I see the ex-premier but doing the charioteer erect, in a very seedy tumbrel, driving off to one of his farms, through the high street of the town, a newly purchased ewe. Imagine Pam turned out—if that be possible to conceive—and, in the leisure of unofficial life, steering a wayward pig through the high street of Tiverton. And yet the Lord Palmerston of Canada could condescend to such a duty without breach of propriety or violation of the rules of decorum. Truly there is something plain, and honest, and unaffected in the home-spun simplicity of this continent, which likes me better than the straitlaced frigidity of English etiquette.

12

IX.

BOSTON.

New York ;
October 18*th.*

It was late on the night of Saturday, September the 24th, when the Vermont Central Railway Company landed me at Boston. I had started very early in the morning from Montreal, whither I proceeded from Cornwall the previous evening, and was pretty well tired out by my long day's ride in the cars of 500 miles. But the country through which my route lay was far more interesting than any I had hitherto seen. I began my railroad journey by passing through the great tubular bridge of which I have already spoken. I had steamed under it already, you will remember, when coming down the St. Lawrence from Prescott to Montreal; and if I was then surprised by the height and span of the colossal arches, I was now as much astonished by the tremendous length of the whole work. Two miles is the estimated extent of the stone and iron work of which its huge structure is composed. The transit from

the northern to the southern bank occupied us many
minutes, and we were in darkness long enough, as a
Yankee remarked, for a Müller to have murdered a
whole compartment-full on any English railway.

A short run brought us to Rouse's Point, the American frontier station, where our baggage was somewhat strictly searched; but to my disappointment,
considering I had taken the trouble to provide myself
with one, passports were not asked for. Whether they
ever have been, or ever will be, I do not know. I can
only say that I have not heard of a single instance in
which they have been required; and I begin to think
that the recent order must have been a *ruse* on the part
of the authorities of the two neighbouring countries for
filling their pockets with fees. My fellow-travellers
to the West had, at the advice of some official, ex-
pended a considerable sum in obtaining certain papers
at Toronto, which they were led to believe would serve
them as passports. Their virtue, however, was never
tested, for no one ever asked for them. Not that I
would lead you to imagine that the general appearance of our party was so intensely respectable as to
ensure us a pass unchallenged anywhere. Tourists,
more particularly the English breed, seldom look respectable; as seen in the *Champs Elysées*, they are
simply disreputable. But nobody that we met carried
anything in the nature of a passport, or had heard of
such an order being enforced; and we came, therefore,

to the disagreeable conclusion that we had been
" smartly" used in this particular, or, as you, perhaps,
would say, swindled.

Vermont is lovely—wonderfully like parts of England ; and that, I dare say, is why I thought so. The
line for some time skirted the shores of the lake
Champlain, one of the prettiest waters in America. I
grudged the rapid passage of its hills and wooded
banks, and almost regretted that I had not come down
it by boat, as do the thousands of excursionists that
every summer flock to its scenery. But time was
precious, and, having so little of it to spare, I was loth
to give up much of it to the country before I had seen
more of the great cities. So the lake passed away ;
and then, for a period of several hours, we wound
through a narrow defile, between two ranges of the
first mountains I had seen on the continent. But
now we were in the midst of something far more like
European scenery. Quiet glens and shadowy dales
succeeded one another at every turn in our course,
reminding me of Devonshire or Wales ; and here and
there a bit of landscape that would recall to my memory
Matlock and Dovedale. The country was never bold
like Switzerland, nor wild like the Scotch Highlands,
but of a quiet pastoral character, very pleasing to the
eye, and particularly refreshing after a fortnight's absence in the flat plains of the West. Then there were
pretty and populous towns in the valleys, and neat little

villages in amongst the hills, and comfort and happiness depicted everywhere—in the pleasant villages at the feet of the slopes, in the well-kept farms upon the rich pastures, in the busy hamlets beside some sparkling rivulet, in the thriving cities upon the Connecticut river. Across the waters of this handsome stream we were in New Hampshire, where the scenery seemed as pretty; but it became dusk soon after we entered the State, and when we were at Concord, the capital, the evening had long closed in. Thence we had to travel through the manufacturing districts of Massachusetts, past Manchester, and Nashua, and Lowell, which smelt very smoky, and very much like Birmingham; and though I was told the country was equally fine, it was much too dark and murky to believe it. But what I had seen of the earlier part of my day's journey led me to agree with the enraptured remarks of my Yankee fellow-passengers that New England was "some punkins"—a pumpkin is an infallible standard of excellence for man or thing—"warn't it?" And I admitted that I should have to change my mind, and allow that America, after all, had some decent scenery, and was, about this district, in less danger than usual of being "whipped" by England. I do not generally humour them when they turn on the bragging tap a little bit too strong. The only way to put a stop to it is to pay them back in their own coin; and if you tell them that Snowdon is twenty miles high, or the

British Museum as big as New York, or that Lord
Palmerston is 120, or that every English bishop has a
landed estate of £500,000 a year, they see at once
that you are up to their game, and drop talking to
you as a fool.

But there were other things to interest me on the
road besides the scenery. One was a novel custom,
which I had several times before observed, of testing
the popular feeling with regard to the coming election,
by taking the votes of the passengers in the trains.
It is constantly done, I hear, before any important
event in which the people have a voice, as a sort of
feeler thrown out by this or that party to try how the
wind blows. The process is extremely simple. A
couple of men traversed the whole length of the train,
asking each man in the various cars for whom he
would give his vote, Lincoln or McClellan, and noting
it accordingly, one taking those for " old Abe," the
other those for " little Mac." I, of course, simply
said I had no vote—a piece of candour on my part
somewhat supererogatory; but I thought it at least
prudent not to claim a vote, and thereby subject myself
to the draft. In the West, near Chicago, and just after
the excitement of the great Democratic Convention, the
votes had been generally in favour of " little Mac.";
but here he was in a sad minority, and those who recorded their votes in his favour were received with
taunts and jeers, showered down upon them most

unmercifully. The tide has turned, and the Young
Napoleon is doomed, like his fancied prototype, to
defeat—and unlike him, to oblivion.

Next me sat a young Presbyterian minister, whose
heart I won by giving him an extremely improbable
interpretation of a verse in a Greek Testament which
he was studying. He was full of information upon
points interesting to me, and willing to impart all he
could, so that I found him a very pleasant companion, and afterwards extremely useful. He held
forth upon the subject of his Church, and the mode of
admission to the status of minister in it, which, from
his account, seems no easy matter; told me that
reading was thoroughly taught, and formed a subject
of final examination for orders—I could not, I said,
congratulate him on the results, though I approved
entirely of the principle, and wished it was so at
home—talked of the marvellous variety of creeds in
his country, and in particular of the Unitarians, into
the head quarters of whose Church, Boston, we were
fast making our way; and made himself generally
agreeable.

Then there was the conductor of the cars to amuse
me. You may wonder what amusement I could draw
from the contemplation of such a seedy picture as is
generally presented by our "guard." But here, that
copper-taking official, who never seems to do anything
else than lock and unlock all the doors, as if he had

a bet on with some sporting party as to how many
times in a minute he will fasten and unfasten every
one of them ; who invariably asks for your ticket
when you least expect it and have just got it safely
down to the bottom of your pocket, and is always out
of the way when the train starts, and cannot be communicated with when it is in motion—here, I say, that
much abused conservator of his passengers' security is
transformed into a well-dressed gentleman in plain
clothes, who indicates, to such of his passengers as are
not short-sighted, the fact of their being in his keeping, by the single word "conductor," in small, neat
characters, upon his coat-collar, or his hat-band, or
his right sleeve, or even his breast-pin. But though
he wears no other external mark of his official character, you will not be left long in doubt as to his
being a man of authority. His power "aboard"—
you are never "in" any conveyance in this country, but
"aboard" it ; you are always asked to go "aboard"
the omnibus ; you are told it is time to get "aboard"
your carriage ; instead of "any more going on" being
shouted at you as it is at home, you are assailed
with "All aboard for" Boston, or other the place of
your destination—well, then, "aboard" his power is
supreme. He is dictator for the time being, as absolute as ever was a ship's captain. But meet him in
the evening, as you probably will, in the coffee-room
of your hotel, and you will find yourself on level

ground with him. And, indeed, if you are civil to him in the cars he will be sociable enough. He spends his time in perambulating the train, sitting down in this car to have a bit of politics with a party of noisy disputants, in that to discuss the crops with a long, lean farmer—they are neither jolly nor fat; here, perhaps, questioning a knot of soldiers, there a couple of smartly dressed ladies, and you may be sure that his eye for beauty is almost always good.

As for the mechanical duties of his office they are quietly and easily discharged—and on this wise. A man's person in America is, like everything else, public property. Should you be wearing anything curious in the way of coats, you will be sure to have two or three fingers and thumbs trying its texture ; and if any one takes a fancy to your trousers he will test them in a similar way, and ask you if you've " a mind to trade them." A friend of mine who has come out in a loud pin consisting of a small nugget in its raw state, has had this novel ornament removed by the hands of a perfect stranger as many as three times in the course of a visit to an hotel bar. I am told that a Yankee has been seen to raise a man's hat from his head to read the maker's name inside. Was there ever such a land of freedom ! Why, at home, it would be assault and battery. But here, as I said before, every visible article of your dress is no more your's than anybody's else. And in accordance with this principle, you wear your ticket in the band of your hat, and the conductor, as he comes round, takes it out as often as necessary, clips, or notches, or changes it, and puts it back. If he cannot readily fix the ticket while your hat is on, he takes it off to do so, and restores it. Nothing is said by him during the operation—nothing ever is in America when unnecessary—nobody pays any attention to his movements. Papers and books are read uninterruptedly, slumbers continued undisturbed, while he proceeds methodically down the car upon his ticket investigation. I have had my ticket notched half a dozen times without the slightest intimation of it.

At our last stopping-place came aboard, as indeed has been the case before reaching any large town to which I have been, a smart fellow with a note-book and pencil, and a handful of neat cards. He asks you your name and hotel; you tell him, and he makes a note of it, takes from you the brass luggage checks which correspond with those you have had affixed to your " pieces " (a plagiarism from the French), gives you a receipt for them and for his charge (something less than a shilling) upon one of his cards—and by the time you want to ascend to your bedroom, you find your luggage there awaiting you. This is what I call comfortable travelling. The baggage-checking system is a great and goodly institution. I cannot imagine why it should not answer at home. Like the sleeping cars, it is undertaken by private companies, independent of, but acting in concert with, the railways. I do not suppose that could be so with us—our railway companies are far too jealous of any stranger's interference. But there seems to be a spirit of co-operation in this country which overrides such petty jealousies. I have before talked of this striking feature, so I will say no more about it now. But I cannot but see that, with all the extravagance of the American principle of "self-help," there is at work, side by side with it, a seemingly paradoxical element of mutual co-operative assistance. And to this co-operation must be attributed, in no small degree, the rapid progress of this youthful country.

I like Boston excessively. Any Englishman, I think, must; it is so much less unlike an English city, and the people are so much less unlike English people, than any city and people I have yet seen in America. The streets do not bore you to death with being straight as arrows, without the slightest variation from what Americans call "the bee line," and the buildings are not squared in aggravating blocks, like rectangular Turin. You cannot imagine what a relief it was to me to find a curve in the High Street, as we have at home in our Regent Street Quadrant; to get comparatively into a region of obtuser angles and less pointed corners; to feel that, if I came into collision with a man's shoulder or a lady's cheekbone,

it would not hurt me. You must have travelled yourself among the new cities of the West to be able to
realise the pleasure of getting back to a country of
respectable age, amidst houses, and men, and things
bearing the impress of time and solidity. The general
features of the city are not in any way particularly
remarkable. It is not a Paris, nor a London; but
there is a good old English stability about the red-
brick buildings, a wealthy comfort in the private
mansions, a luxurious display in the windows of the
stores, and a pleasaut undulation in the ground on
which the city stands, that compensate for the lack of
a Tuilleries or a St. Paul's, and, to my mind, make
Boston a very delightful city. But, after all, I suspect its chief feature of recommendation in my eyes
was its similarity to an English town; and if there
had only been a little smoke in the atmosphere, and
none of those beautiful Virginian creepers twining up
the faces of the private houses, I could have imagined
myself at home again in one of our quiet, old-fashioned
cities.

Sunday was spent in company with my Presbyterian
friend, in a visit to two of the popular preachers of the
day, with a pleasant afternoon's walk between the
services in the chief streets and the park. The evening
sermon was delivered at a curious place of worship
tenanted by members of the Congregationalist faith—
do not ask me what that is;—and the immediate

object of the particular meeting was to collect funds for
the relief of sufferers in the war, and the families of
those slain in one of Sheridan's engagements in the
Shenandoah Valley. It was an impressive scene. The
lists of casualties had not been issued. Several thousands were known to have fallen ; and fathers, mothers,
sisters, and brothers of those whose regiments had
been in the fight, had flocked together, to hear per-
chance from some unofficial source the tidings which
the War Office had kept back. Several besides the
minister addressed the anxious crowd. There was no
cant, no hypocrisy; nothing but an earnest faith in
the justice of the cause for which such floods of blood
were given, and prayers as earnest for its ultimate
success. I have said but little of the war as yet, because the fact is that I had been so many hundred
miles away from its scene, that its effect, though painfully visible even at the remotest point of my Western
excursion, was always counteracted by something which
seemed to take the poignancy from its sting. In the
cities there were always to be seen at every turn
maimed limbs and emaciated frames, charred embers
of humanity; but the sight of these blood-chilling
spectacles told with little effect upon the rough aus-
terity of the Western character. Farmers would break
into a savage growl that their sons or their labourers
had all gone down South ; merchants would utter a rude
murmur that their clerks had all enlisted; but corn

was high, and money was rolling into Chicago at a
pace which before the war was unknown.   But now,
at Boston, I was amongst another people.   Near
enough to the scene of the fighting to feel the shock
of each battle's struggle, and in the midst of hearts
that beat with horror at the terrible sacrifices required
by the God of war.   I listened attentively to the
various speakers, much moved by the quiet earnestness
of their words, and the pious sympathy of their hearers,
and gave my mite with abundant readiness for the
widows and orphans whose cause was being pleaded.

The next day I was introduced by my two fellow-
passengers from England, whom I met here by arrangement, to a well-known Boston man, Mr. Loring.   He
made his fortune at the Bar, where he attained a very
high position, and has now retired to live at ease upon the
earnings of his early labours.   Nothing could exceed the
civility with which he treated me, a perfect stranger to
him, simply upon the introduction of my companions,
who carried a letter to him from an English friend.   He
took us to all the chief objects of interest in the city :
to the Court House, the Museum, the Public Library,
and the Law Court ; then to his club, an extremely
comfortable establishment, where he put down our
names for admission, and in the most courteous and
delicate manner gave orders that any meals we might
desire should be at his expense ; and, finally, he invited
us to spend a day with him at his country seat on the

sea-shore, about twenty miles from Boston, which we
did; and a very pleasant day it was.   The train soon
ran us down to Salem, a fashionable watering-place of
the Bostonians, and at the next station, where we dis-
mounted, we found in waiting for us a handsome carriage and pair, sent by our host to take us up to his
house.   The gate leading to his property was close
by, and thence we had a most lovely drive through a
prettily wooded glen, resembling those sweet dells that
abound in the Scottish Highlands, and at the end of it
we emerged upon a low rocky promontory, running
out into the bay of Salem, on the margin of which
stood one of the prettiest summer residences conceivable.   There our host received us, and after an introduction to his family, we started with him to survey
his grounds.   They were very tastefully laid out.
Nature had done the greater portion of the work for
him; what artificial additions he had made were in excellent harmony with the original. A few skilful arrangements of loose boulder stones, a wild creeper dexterously
trained, a natural cavern ingeniously taken advantage of,
sufficed to enhance the beauty of this leaf from Nature's
book, and afford a specimen of landscape gardening
which I have rarely seen equalled.   His farm was as
neat as his garden.   His cattle of good breed, some of
them fine Alderneys.   His pigs, to my surprise Suf-
folk, so clean and sweet, that I felt half inclined to
embrace them for old acquaintance sake.   His stables,

not less neat and wholesome, so arranged as to keep
his horses' heads to the daylight, instead of blinding
their eyes by the ordinary confinement of their view
to a hundred square inches of blank wall.   His barn
and yards perfect models of what farm premises should
be.

It seemed strange to me, I can hardly say why, to
find an American ruralising in this way exactly like
our country gentlemen.   I was not prepared for anything half so English.   I came out with the idea that
everybody lived in an hotel, rich and poor alike, and
as for English squires in America, I should sooner have
looked for a Harrow and Eton cricket match.   But
here was the model English gentleman reproduced in
all his ease and luxury, surrounded by the comforts of
an elegant house, a large circle of friends and visitors,
carriages and horses for the pretty drives in the neighbourhood, yachts and sailing boats for the bay, and
spending his leisure hours of relaxation from the cares
of public life in just the sort of model farming
which pleases the pride and pilfers the pockets of the
genuine squire in Old England.   Alderman Mechi
would hardly guess, perhaps, that he had a disciple
amongst the Yankees.   I do not suppose the number
of such country gentlemen on this continent is anything but very small.   I can safely assert that I have
met with extremely few who could by any stretch of
imagination be mistaken for that true type of good

manners and good breeding which is to be seen so frequently at home. The Yankee may be decently educated, intelligent, affable, courteous, but, with all this, I must confess it, he will seldom be a gentleman. There is always something about him which prevents his being classified as such, some vulgarity in his look, his dress, his gesture, his language, that stamps him as unworthy of the name. It is impossible to define precisely what the several distinguishing marks of his degeneracy are. A " boots," you know, can tell from the general appearance of the leathers which he has to clean whether their respective owners are gentlemen or not, but I dare say he would find it difficult to describe to you what the different signs are upon which he founds his judgment. So with me and these Yankees. In the same way as a public-school man is generally to be told by his fellows, though the shades of distinction may be so fine that they could give no definite explanation of the exact grounds of their decision, so I am unable to lay down in any comprehensive statement the precise method by which I arrive at the general proposition that no Yankee is a gentleman. The voice and intonation, however much it grates upon the ear, I put out of the question as a national peculiarity which ought to have little weight in the estimation of individual character. But there are other points which grate as much upon the senses, of which I can only say this, that I am sure they would lead *you* to the same conclusion.

13

A friend of mine, a good scholar and an ever ready wit, who emigrated to New Zealand, complained in piteous language of the lack of any educated ears upon which he could crack his classical jokes. I do not urge the same complaint against the Americans, nor have I the same title to do so. But I must say that any Englishman who has had a University education would find that he had little in common with the ordinary run of Americans, nothing sympathetic between their ideas and his. You may imagine, then, what a pleasure it was to be in the presence of one in whom we could not recognise any of these disparaging indications which we had found so distressingly numerous. With Mr. Loring it was far otherwise, and the few hours of conversation which we had with him that day passed as agreeably, and I hope, profitably, as any I passed upon the Continent.

The chief subject of discussion was the war. It had a painful interest for Mr. Loring—he had a son, a grandson, a nephew, and four cousins then at the front. But he told us he was no exception to the rest of his countrymen in New England; he could point out a street in Boston from every house in which had gone forth at least one member of the family to fight for the cause they upheld. I have before hinted that my innocent confidence in the 'Times' had in this respect, as in many others, led me into the most grievous errors. You have been told how surprised I

was to find in the army of the West so small a proportion of foreigners comparatively with what I had
anticipated; and if you consider the enormous number
of German and other immigrants who have settled
here and enjoyed the privileges of their citizenship,
you will see that the alien settlers have scarcely turned
out with the alacrity that might have been expected
of them, in defence of the government under which
they live.   But I believe the most inconsiderate par-
tisans of the South will allow that the Western army
is composed of the proper stuff, and therefore it is
rather with the army of the East that I wish to deal.
Now, I am writing this in Washington, which is the
head quarters of that army, and I have had already
some means of judging of the material of which it is
composed.   There are Irish in it, no doubt; there are
English, there are French and Germans in the ranks;
but the proportion is surprisingly less than you and I
have been led to believe.   Nine or ten hundred dollars
bounty-money paid down, and high wages besides, are
enough in themselves to attract from every quarter of
the globe the waifs and strays of humanity.   War is
a game of chance, and all who have nothing to lose
can afford to have a throw in it.   A flesh-wound or
an attack of rheumatism may send them to the rear
undamaged, and a place in the lists of the Invalid
Corps is a comfortable sinecure.   But if you will not
admit that the Northerners themselves have borne any

part in the brunt of war, how will you explain the fact that the merchant's office, the tradesman's warehouse, the lawyer's chambers, the colleges and schools, are deserted by their ordinary tenants; and the very business of the Treasury, the Post Office, the State department, nay, even the War Office itself, is of necessity entrusted to female heads and hands? If you deny that the Federals have done anything more than provide the money wherewith to bait the hook for alien mercenaries, what is the meaning of the mourning garments in which half the nation is clad? what is the explanation of the widows' weeds that confront you at every step? It used to be the boast of the liberal-minded Englishman that he would hear the two sides of every question before he ventured to deliver judgment. Has he now forgotten the good old maxim, *Audi alteram partem?* Have the influential journals of the day, in their admiration of a heroism, which the Federals as fully admit and honour, allowed us to see any but one side of this great question, and that painted in such extravagant colours as the 'Index' itself, its recognised advocate, will not condescend to use? I do not mean to subscribe to all that has been done by the North. The question is far too vast to enter upon in a simple letter; but I say that the truth of the history of the last four years has been systematically kept from us by those from whom we had a right to hear it.

Mr. Loring talked of this with emotion. " Some

of my countrymen," he said, "seemed to think that
this party feeling and party writing was due as a
measure of retaliation for the empty rhodomontade of
the 'New York Herald;' but the comparison between
the power and influence of that journal and that of
one like the 'Times,' is ludicrous." The 'Herald' is
known to be conducted by a man of no principle whatever—an outcast from our shores and all respectable
society here; and, for all I know, his staff of paper-
defiling underlings are men of like origin and character. The paper circulates, but nobody believes a
word he reads there. It sells for its size, the amount
of reading contained in it, and the number and raci-
ness of its advertisements; but it exercises no more
influence over the thinking portion of the people than
does the 'Family Herald' or the 'Record' over the
actions of the British Government. The 'Times'
holds a very different position. It has attained such
a power now, that it no longer is the mere exponent
of the views and opinions of the day, but leads and
moulds men's minds at its will. The Americans know
this, and weigh every word of it accordingly.

Our host was most earnest and impressive in his
advocacy of the Federal cause. His quiet easy
eloquence seemed to carry us along with him in his
exposition of the origin of the war, and the doctrines
involved in its justification. He proclaimed the question to be none of expediency, or finance, or internal

economy, nor even one of fundamental construction of
the Constitution or organic law, but one underlying
and beyond all these—the question of national life—
the question whether the national union should be
preserved, and the people continue to exist as a great
and independent nation capable of self-government
and secure from foreign aggression, or be split up and
dismembered into any unforeseen number of weak
and distracted municipalities, with clashing interests
and embittering jealousies, to end eventually, perhaps,
in military despotism, as their only refuge from anarchy
and perpetual war—the question, as he subsequently
put it in a great speech in Boston, " Whether twenty
million of freemen in arms against four millions of
traitors under the rule of three hundred thousand
slaveholders should ignominiously kneel as suppliants
at their feet, to ascertain upon what terms they would
condescend to resume their ancient sway in the national Councils ; or what guarantees they would demand for the perpetuation and extension of their
infernal traffic in flesh and blood :" and when the
venerable orator closed his address to us by asserting
that he was ready to lay down his life to-morrow for
the cause, if he thought that the individual sacrifice
would advance it, I felt that I was in the presence of
a sober earnestness and devotional patriotism for which
the Federals get little credit.

But I must leave this subject.   After a look at his

son's charger, which had become quite unnerved by
the long list of bloody engagements and the sufferings
from exposure through which he had passed, and was
now being nursed at home in a pretty paddock near
the house, we said good-bye to our host, and were
soon again in Boston. Before I take you with me to
Washington, I must tell you that we paid a visit to
Cambridge, the seat of the University of Harvard. It
lies about three miles out of the city, across one of
the long low bridges which cross the Charles River,
in a pretty situation, amongst handsome timber and
neat looking residences. The college itself is utterly
unworthy of comparison with its English namesake.
There is a library and a chapel, but of neither is the
architecture very grand, and the collegiate buildings
consist of about half a dozen detached blocks, in a
style perhaps less impressive than that peculiarly unimposing college, Downing. The lecture-hall is large,
but ugly. Dining-hall there is none; nor Senate-
house, nor "High," nor "King's Parade," nor bed-
makers; and, generally, I should say that the visitor
from the English Universities would not be particularly impressed with the American imitation.

We called on some friends whose acquaintance we
had made, and saw the sort of rooms in which the
undergraduates reside. Some of them "room" in
college, some in lodgings, as with us; but they seem
to mess together at certain of the boarding-houses

which surround the college; and at six o'clock, when
we called, our friends had just had tea.   This did not
sound to us much like the English idea of University
life.   The students did not appear to have any amusement beyond that of loafing, and loafing in particular
about the porch of the Post Office—for letters are
never delivered here, and what you want in this
country you go for (or without)—no cricket, no rowing,
nor racquets; only loafing, and tea at six!   What a
picture of University education!   It really was most
melancholy to see these poor youths stalking unhappily
about and finishing their bread and butter at the door
of their mess-house, in the idea, no doubt, that they
were at least following, if not improving upon, the
system of University life in old England.   There
were no "gates."   How could an American citizen
be subjected to such a restraint?   No sacred grass.
Who should keep an American citizen off it?   They
were free to go and do as they pleased, how, when,
and where they pleased, and the result seemed to me
to be that they did nothing.   The only thing that
could have transported me mentally to the banks of
the Cam was the announcement that there was morning chapel at seven; only that I was at the same time
told that the service was Unitarian—I do not know
what that is like, but it sounds as if it lasted much
longer than ours does as read at " morning chapels"—
and that it came directly after breakfast, which was

at half-past six.—I do not know what that may be like either, but I cannot fancy anything more unlike the customs of either Cam or Isis.

Further on is Mount Auburn, the cemetery for the city of Boston. It is a lovely spot—almost as beautiful as *Père la Chaise*—ornamented with handsome timber of every variety, and decked with all the extravagance with which the French decorate their burial-grounds. The flowers on and around the monuments were tasty and elegant. All was in harmony, and not vulgar. I have since seen the cemetery at Baltimore, and that again is as admirable. The burial-ground seems to me to be one of the most conspicuous ornaments of the large cities of this continent. It is invariably well planted, tastily laid out, though possibly, to the English eye, too highly ornamental, and well cared-for; and, like the great cemetery at Munich, it usually becomes one of the fashionable promenades of the citizens. Death, in this country, has little of the attendant awe which its presence awakens with us. Possibly the Americans are right in discouraging the mysterious repugnance to the sight of it in the death-chamber which the English habits too readily, I think, foster. The funeral here takes place often on the day following the death, more generally the second day after, seldom later. Invitations to attend are not issued, as our custom is. All who care to pay the last tribute of respect to their departed friend do so. Those who are nearly related or intimately connected with the family come in black; others in their ordinary dress. The only mourning provided by the officials is a small band of crape for the arm. The corpse lies in its coffin uncovered, in a convenient room; and there all who attend take their last look at the lifeless features. This done, the lid is soldered down, and the coffin is placed in a hearse, which is either altogether open or has sides of glass. The funeral procession is rather a motley one: the variety of the costumes and the vehicles detracts from the solemnity of sorrow, which, notwithstanding the dissipated looks of our mutes, accompanies an English funeral. Women, too, follow the body to the grave; but they do everything in America which the men do, from wearing their hair cut short and close to the head to gum-chewing and platform declamation.

Of course I saw Bunker's Hill, and the great monument commemorative of the defeat of the Britishers, as I had previously seen the sacred oak under which Washington first unsheathed his sword in defence of his country; and though I could not see anything much like a hill upon the spot, yet the height of the monument made up for the want of any elevation in the ground; and from the top of it there was a magnificent view to be had of Boston mapped out beneath us, and the docks and the shipping beyond, and the bright blue sea in the distance; but I must have wearied you with attempts at scenic descriptions, and so I will pass on to the Navy Yard. We had, at first, some difficulty in getting admission; but when once through the gates with the help of an introduction from the landlord of our hotel, we met with every attention and civility from the officers on guard. There was plenty of life there, you may be sure. The exigencies of the war have raised from the earth, as it were by magic, a gigantic Vulcan's workshop in the midst of a city, where four years ago, I suppose, a gun or a shell was a nine days' wonder. Our time was much too short for our own pleasure, as well as that of the captain of the guard, who was anxious that we should see everything—not exactly everything, however, because we were not permitted to look at one of the new Monitors which was then being finished for service. Still we managed to get near enough to her to see that her plates were not solid, but composed of five separate layers, a plan which I believe has been found by us far inferior to the solid plate, though I suppose rapidity of construction is gained by the American method, and that is the object at which they aim. She certainly was the queerest looking craft that I ever set eyes upon. You have seen them represented in the ' Illustrated London News,' and with accuracy too, only that they are actually lower in the water than those portraits of them would lead you to imagine. This particular one of which I speak showed less than a foot above the water-line, so that practically no part of her was visible but the two ugly turrets in her centre. What a life it must be below ! How any man can be found willing to sink himself in this sort of aggravated salmon-box, and gasp at the bottom of a funnel for the few cubic inches of air that can be conveyed down it, with shots playing all around him from an enemy who cannot be seen, and guns above his head that are pretty sure to burst, and torpedoes beneath his feet, and what the Yankees call " a right smart chance " of swamping if it comes on to blow, is one of the wonders of the world. How the spirit of Nelson must have coloured on receiving the first telegram of these revolutions in the service ! A hurried view round the forges, the castings both of guns and shell, and a glimpse at the finishing shops, and the scene of activity on the quay which was covered with " Parrott " guns, or "soda-water bottles," as they are called, from the absurd similarity of their form, and, as I ventured to add, equally brittle nature ; and then we had to leave for New York. We did so with regret. The place was more congenial to our natures than any other we had visited. It will always live in my memory as the first town on this continent in which a lady, Canadian or American, thanked me for giving up to her my seat in a street car, and the place where I first learnt that a Yankee could be a gentleman.

X.

WASHINGTON.

It was late on Saturday, October 1st, when I reached Washington. I had intended to stop the night in Baltimore, but saw so little there worth stopping for, that I determined to push on at once to objects of greater interest. Our party had left Boston four days before by the night mail for New York. The distance of more than 200 miles was very easily got over, for I had a capital berth in a very comfortable sleeping-car, and I slept in perfect unconsciousness of what was going on, unaware even of the presence in the opposite berth of two very pretty girls, dozing quietly in front of me, till I was roused, about seven o'clock in the morning, by the attendant of the car, who brought me my boots, and told me that we were in New York. I looked out, and found that our train had become a series of street-cars. It had been split up into segments, two or three cars in a division, to each of which was attached a team of half-a-dozen horses, who rattled us down the centre of the street, through which the rails are carried far into the heart of the city. The time that was occupied in passing to the depôt I spent in a tolerably satisfactory toilet. It would be absurd to expect much of the comfort of an ordinary dressing-room on board either a train or a steamboat. I was thankful enough for what means of ablution I could get in the little box attached to the car; and though it might seem strange to you to meet a railway-carriage coming down Oxford Street, with a lot of men towelling their faces, and putting on their coats upon the platform at one end of it, and a posse of women polishing up their back hair at the other, I can assure you that I took to it all as naturally as if I had been brought up to the system from my vac-cination. This is something *like* independence, if you will. Arrived at the depôt, I had nothing to do but to walk up to the hotel, "The Fifth Avenue," of world-wide fame, and sit down to breakfast. My luggage troubled me not; it was checked for the hotel, and would follow me before I wanted it. What, I ask, is the just cause or impediment why this simplest of sys-tems should not be imported into England? If you do not approve of the idea of making your toilette in a public street, at least you must admit that the Ame-ricans are wise in their attempts to diminish the fatigue of a long night journey; and parents who have their scruples need not let their daughters sleep in the same compartment with a couple of young gentlemen. But these things excite no wonder in the States; and though I find it hard to reconcile myself to this open abhorrence of prudery, I cannot see that any one is much the worse for it.

I shall say nothing about New York now, except that my first three days in the city aroused my loudest approbation of its grandeur. We had Washington to see, and Baltimore, and Philadelphia; and so I will leave New York for the present. The cars to Baltimore were far inferior to those on the Boston line. The train was crammed with soldiers going down to the front, redolent of dirt, tobacco-smoke, and bad language. At four o'clock in the morning we were driving in sections of cars through Philadelphia. It seemed an enormous city, and so we afterwards found it. Thence we pushed on to Baltimore. I had been dozing again, as well as the jolting of the cars would permit me to do, when I was roused by the stoppage of the train, which was again broken up into segments, and shunted on to a steam ferry that was to take us over a small inlet of the sea. And here it was that we first came in visible contact with the presence of war. A Confederate raid had, in the early part of the year, been made upon the country around, with a view of getting at Baltimore; and strong guards had been necessarily maintained there ever since. So here, when

we were moved on board this ferry, a detachment of
Federal soldiers boarded our cars.   Two stationed
themselves, with bayonets intercrossed, at either end
of each car, while the officers perambulated amongst
the passengers, and scrutinised their prisoners.   Whether this imposing manœuvre was for the purpose of
detecting spies or deserters, or both, I could not satisfactorily make out.   One soldier amongst our passengers, who, I suppose, had not his proper papers about
him, was marched off under arrest to the guard-room
when we reached the opposite bank.   But I presume
that we neither looked sharp enough to be spies, nor
dirty enough to be deserters, for nobody put any questions to any of our party, and at the other side of the
bay our blue-coated custodians left us to go our way
in peace.   The same ceremonious scrutiny was repeated
before we reached Baltimore, at a similar ferry, and at
Baltimore itself we found the station in the hands of a
regiment of Federal troops, who stuck themselves about
the platform with crossed bayonets in everybody's way,
and created an enormous amount of obstruction and
consequent confusion, with, so far as I could see, the
most insignificant results; and we finally left the station in Indian file, through a double line of these pro-
voking bayonets that seemed a good deal too near my
eyes to be agreeable, deeply impressed with the plea-
sures of living under martial law.   But Baltimore is
rank "Secesh," and requires an iron rod to rule

her; and she has got what she wants, with a vengeance.

People told me I should find Baltimore dirty, and I was not disappointed. Good Republicans say it is unclean because it is a Southern city, and all Southern cities are unclean. Whether the general proposition be true I do not know; at any rate, Washington is no exception. But the dirt of Baltimore is of a higher and more ancient order. It is a queer old town, all ups and downs, and odd angles. The houses are chiefly brick, which is red, and the soil of the neighbourhood is red, and the mud in the streets is red, and the negro women's favorite colour is red. The day was unfavorable, I admit, for it rained pretty steadily, and the water rushed down the slopes into the lower levels, and there accumulated in a lot of stagnant pools, which are crossed by stepping-stones for pedestrians. The science of driving through the intervals between them is thus reduced to a nicety that the Four-in-hand Club might envy. It "whips" even that of driving in an American city without losing your wheels in a street-car track— a feat which the natural clumsiness, or, as Mr. Train thinks, the wilful intolerance, of our London omnibus drivers upon his tramway in the Bayswater Road, failed to accomplish. They certainly manage to keep their wheels on in America, but you ought to have the hide of a rhinoceros to stand the jarring and jolting of the wheels as they scrape along and catch in the rails.

14

There were several things to be seen in the city and the neighbourhood. There was Barnum's Hotel, our abiding place, and a national monument or two, and a pretty cemetery, and a park and ornamental gardens, and quays and wharves and storehouses, and, what interested me as much as anything, a public library and lecture hall, called "The Peabody Institute." This was by no means the first of these institutions we had met with. The public library is one of the chief objects of interest in every city of the Free States. It is only one branch of the grand system of free education which has made the Americans what they are. The library is, of course, open to all. Like everything else in the country, the poorest citizen has as much right to its volumes as the wealthiest. It has no inner tabernacle, to which a respectable householder's introduction can alone give admission. My innocent question whether no ticket was required of the applicants for books, no credentials of some sort or kind, was received by the librarian with astonishment. But a glance at my whiskers stamped me as English, and he smiled and explained. One thing that has struck me as much or perhaps more than the extent of the social freedom of the Americans, is the absence of abuse of it. A Yankee labourer in conversation with his master is on terms of perfect equality with him, yet he never presumes upon his master's courtesy to descend to impertinence. The servant in her proper sphere is respectful to her mistress, though outside of it she is as great a woman as her lady. So here in these public institutions everything is open to the hands and eyes of everybody, but no one takes advantage of his right to injure or abstract. I am afraid this is almost more than can be said for us. The Library of the British Museum, close as it is, has not once only had its volumes damaged by its privileged readers. Public exhibitions have to be tended by guardians of the public peace, who in America can be dispensed with with impunity. But larcenies and petty thefts are crimes of rare occurrence in the States. People are not driven by want to such methods of earning a livelihood; and necessity, which is the mother of crime, as well as of invention, is staved off by the demand for labour. Peelers, save in New York, are as rare as beggars; and of the latter I have seen fewer during my sojourn in the States than I should in a ten minutes' walk in Oxford Street.

Baltimore, you know, is celebrated all the world over for two excellent characteristics—the beauty of its women, and its canvas-backed ducks. Of the former I saw but little, for the rain kept them indoors; and though it might have suited the latter, they were out of season. But of the ladies, I will only say that I do not see how there can be much improvement upon the general good looks that meet me in every city, East and West alike. They are a little too Frenchified, perhaps, but they wear no crinoline, and that is ever-lastingly to their credit, besides adding immensely to their general appearance. If a lady has a good figure, why should she not let those who have an eye for form know it? Why must she metamorphose herself into a pyramidal cone, or an indecently tall mushroom? I cannot conceive how a lady can watch another into a carriage or an omnibus and not vote with the aboli-tionists.

I left Baltimore in the evening, and by supper-time I was at Willard's Hotel in Washington. The station here was as strongly guarded as at Baltimore, and especial note was taken by the officers of every passenger that alighted; but I was allowed to pass un-questioned. There was a tremendous crowd at Wil-lard's; more than three fourths of them military men, the rest government clerks, officials, and newspaper correspondents, and here and there a Congress-man or two, always men of great expectorations. All the time I remained in Washington, every day and any hour of the day, were to be seen in the hall and about the porch the same faces that met my view on my first arrival at the hotel. And such a set of "loafers" no man elsewhere ever saw. I thought that this thoroughly Yankee occupation was carried to a high state of perfection in New York, but no "loafing" that I saw there could compare with what went on

from early morning to early morning in the vicinity of
Willard's. If I saw one man standing by the doorway and spitting at a stone in the pavement I saw a
couple of hundred. Go out and come in when I would,
there were always the same heels upon the tops of the
chairs along the pathway under the awning, the same
hands turning over the leaves of all the novels on the
bookstall in the hall without ever purchasing one of
them, the same readers in the journal room, the same
loungers in the barber's shop, the same idlers talking
to the coat-and-parcel-checker, the same contro-
versialists disputing hotly with the landlord or his
clerks behind the bar. The universal theme was the
war in connection with the approaching election.
The movements of the army were telegraphed and
rumoured in contradictory language a hundred times a
day, and each new report was a fresh battle-field for
angry argument. Grant's tactics and Lee's stratagems,
Sheridan's raids and Sherman's march, were fought
over and discussed *ad nauseam*. Nobody's conception
of the next day's news ever turned out correct; nobody's prophecy of the next movement was ever veri-
fied; nobody's statement of the last proved true; and
by the time I left the city I was thoroughly sick of
the vague and fruitless rumours which the newspaper
correspondents delighted in circulating, and most
heartily disgusted with the glorious uncertainty of
war.

Washington now is nothing more nor less than a gigantic military depôt. The pavement is crowded with uniforms; Paris cannot show half as many. Every open piece of ground—and there are lots of them, for the city is not half finished—is converted into a camp; every square is built over with Aldershot huts; every other house is a military storehouse, or a hospital, or a recruiting office, or a provost-martial's quarters, or a branch of the Sanitary Commission, or a temporary barrack. All day long, and often all night, the centre of the chief streets is occupied with an interminable chain of ambulances and military waggons, carrying down supplies to the front. Strings of mules, I am afraid to say how long, returning for fresh waggons, street cars crammed with troops, detachments of deserters being marched down again to their regiments, squads of prisoners being brought in, sick and wounded on their way to the hospitals, regiments going out, and regiments coming in—such are the present sights to be seen in the High Street of Washington. Go and stand five minutes at the door of Willard's Hotel, and you will get some little idea of what it costs to carry on a war on such a colossal scale. Sleep there for ten nights, and hear the dull, distant rumbling of the eternal ambulances, and the everlasting tramp of horses' feet, and you will wonder no longer at the fearful debt which the North is heaping upon her shoulders.

You may imagine, from what I have said of the

aspect of the city, that the present is no time for seeing Washington as it was. The public buildings are still there (notwithstanding the recent alarm for their safety on the occasion of the last Confederate raid); but the city itself is so changed, that it is not fair to judge it by its present condition. I hope this is the case; for I must say that my anticipations of the city are woefully disappointed. Dickens, I remember, has likened it to the worst portions of Tottenham Court Road, but I thought that twenty years would have made the comparison inapplicable; yet I believe I can give you at this day no better description of its general aspect than by telling you what Dickens told his readers, that it is wonderfully like that disreputable thoroughfare. Only imagine it widened to five or six times its actual breadth, pull down the houses on the western side, and in their place, with naked intervals, suppose a number of wooden and brick hovels, very low, and indescribably dirty. Pull up the pavement of the road, and down the middle run a double line of rails; plant a few trees along the edge of the pathway, which must be of gravel on the western side and uneven bricks upon the other; make the gutters nowhere in particular, and mud everywhere; and you have the High Street of Washington, when it rains. Take the same imaginary details, and in place of mud conceive an Indian dust-storm and a Cologne smell; and you have the High Street of Washington, when it is dry. Imagine a lot of similar thoroughfares intersecting each other at right angles, with buildings fewer and further between, every house straggling away from its neighbours, each side of every street ashamed of being seen in company with the other; break up the several thoroughfares with unoccupied open spaces, hidden with hoardings like Smithfield Market just now, or unconcealed eyesores like Leicester Square; and add mud, or dust and smells, according to the weather; and you have the rest of Washington, wet or dry.

But, you will say, there are the public buildings. Surely, the political Capital of the United States must contain something in the way of architecture not altogether contemptible. So it does. There is the Capitol, of which we have heard so much; the White House, of which, perhaps, we have heard even more; the Treasury, War Office, Patent Office, Post Office, and one or two decent churches; but they are all so many pearls scattered about in a pigstye. They are all twice as far as they ought to be from one another, connected by the meanest thoroughfares, mean not in breadth, but buildings. I have often thought, as I have been watching the hands of a shop clock from the window of a cab stuck fast in a dead block near Shoreditch, and wondering what my chances were of catching the Great Eastern express, how grand the city of London would look, let alone the facility of locomotion, if all the streets were at least as wide again as

WASHINGTON.   217

Portland Place or St. James's Street. I have now
seen Washington; and henceforth, however deep my
cab may be in vans, and brewers' carts, and waggons,
I shall be more moderate in my demands for extravagant width of roadway. The thoroughfares of Washington are so preposterously broad, that the houses are
dwarfed to insignificance. The very ten-storied monsters of " Auld Reekie" would look like dolls' houses
along their sides. The fearful traffic of Cheapside
would be lost in the middle of them. Washington is
crammed with residents. The army itself adds its tens
of thousands, and agents, sutlers, and hangers-on innumerable; and, for all that, Washington looks to me
like Pall Mall in September. There is a dreary, desolate vacation aspect about the unsociable breadth of its
thoroughfares, about the unoccupied wastes into which
every other street takes you, about the disjointed,
straggling hugeness of the place, that gives it the appearance of a big deserted village, abandoned before it
was half finished.

But I suppose you want to hear something of the
Capitol. Well, its situation is magnificent—nothing
in the world could be finer. Planted on the edge of
a lofty eminence that looks across the Potomac to the
distant mountains of Virginia, it commands a grand
comprehensive view of the city and the river beyond,
and the beautiful hills behind. The slopes of the bluff
on which it stands are thickly studded with handsome

trees, and the immediate neighbourhood of the building is tastily laid out in ornamental gardens, which are
at all times a fashionable promenade. Looking up to
it from the end of Pennsylvania Avenue—a broad,
straight thoroughfare, nearly two miles in length—you
could not fail to be struck with the imposing aspect of
the Capitol, raising its huge white dome high into the
air from out the dense foliage of its gardens, and
towering above the low habitations of the city with
unrivalled grandeur. The building is principally of pure
white marble, clean as driven snow. The columns are
Corinthian; the massive steps by which it is approached
are as yet but half finished, as, indeed, may be said of
almost every part of it, for workmen were busy all
over it when we paid our visit, and, with the present
rates of wages and scarcity of labour, many months
must elapse before it can be completed. . The dome is
vast, but beautifully proportioned, so that its elegant
curve gives grace and character to the whole edifice.
It is not of stone: the Yankees have been guilty of a
piece of native trickery, for the dome forms the cap to
a sort of cylinder built of inferior material, while the
semblance of solid masonry is preserved by an enormous white iron screen, moulded into the form of the
ordinary base of the cathedral dome, which is carried
round the internal cylinder at a considerable distance
from it. Ruskin and all who hate shams would boil
with indignation at the deception; but until you as-

cend the dome, it is perfect. Whether the actual
vault of the rotunda is larger than that of St. Peter's,
the Yankee of whom I inquired did not pretend to
say; all he knew about it was that it was a good deal
bigger than the dome of St. Paul's, which did not shut
me up, as he expected, because I explained to him that
these two were really very much of a size. The rotunda beneath it is certainly very fine, but the pictures
around are by no means worthy of their position. I
feel that I am descending somewhat to the statistics of
a Murray's Hand-book, so I will not trouble you with
details about the two houses, which are something like
ours, and the new Congress Hall, which will be like
the French Chambers, and the corridors and lobbies,
which are, apparently, like neither, but promise to be
elegant, though perhaps too florid. The nigger who
showed us over the houses, and pointed out how the
members sat, said he wished we could come down some
day when there was what he called a "'nation row"
on—he guessed we should have "a good time."

"Does not the President keep order?" said I.

"Guess he tries to keep 'em quiet; but, golly, it's a
perfect Babel!"

From the gallery round the dome there is a
wonderful view. That from the Superga at Turin is
finer only because the mountains are capped with snow.
At Washington, of course, their actual height above
the sea-level is comparatively with the Alps that of an

ant-hill, but their relative height to the objects in the landscape is by no means insignificant. As we saw them they were capped, not with snow, but snow-white camps, jotted about in broken lines and clustering settlements as far as the eye could reach; and from the summit of every height floated the Federal flag over the outlying forts that encircle the great city and its suburbs. Below us, and, as it were, beneath our feet, lay the broad waters of the Potomac and the distant bluffs of Arlington, and nearer still the straggling houses of the city, and out of the city across the valley and up one of the far-off slopes wound a long train of ambulances, coiling itself away like some mighty serpent into the forests of Virginia.

I have no time to tell you of the library; or the heating and cooling apparatus, an ingenious engine with a monster fan, which can renew the whole atmosphere of either house with hot or cold currents in less than five minutes. Nor can I stay to talk of the Smithsonian Museum, which appeared to preserve little else than nasty things bottled in spirits; or the Patent Office, which is decorated after the fashion of an Egyptian temple, and seems to contain a model of every mechanical movement or device that has ever been invented since the days of Tubal Cain, all unarranged and uncatalogued, every glass case a perfect chaos of indistinguishable confusion, looking as if it had just been shaken up by a mischievous schoolboy "making hay." Then there was the Post Office, too, like all American post offices, a large imposing building, with its many rows of glass-fronted pigeon-holes, which are rented by the residents for the deposit of their letters ; for the Post Office delivers none outside its walls, because the price of labour is so high that the stamp would not cover the wages of a perambulating letter-carrier, and you cannot make a pigeon of a Yankee as you can of the underpaid British postman. There was the Treasury, too, a handsome edifice, through which we were conducted by the Under-Secretary, a representative of the far-known race of Smiths, who, whether they be simple Smiths with an "i," or aspiring Smiths with a "y," or vain enough to add an "e," seem to evince on this continent the same regenerative powers of keeping up their kind as they exhibit at home, and, in fact, are a second S.P.G., Society for the Propagation of their Genus, wherever the English language is spoken.

The Treasury is most elegantly furnished. Every office is handsomely fitted, papered, and carpeted. I never saw any rooms that looked less like work, or more removed from the conventional high stool and ruler. And who do you think were the clerks ? Six hundred young ladies in bunchy back hair and Spanish bodices. The ordinary staff of clerks had been more than half absorbed in the sterner duties of the war, and this, like many of the other State departments, was now in great part entrusted to the sharp wits of the Yankee women. Some of them were youthful widows, some poor orphan girls, whom the battle-field had bereft of their only support, a husband's or a father's hand. Of the capability for the work committed to them I have no doubt, for a Yankee girl's schooling is most thorough and complete; but on more than one of their desks in front of the fair face of the occupant I observed a telltale nosegay, which I pointed out to our conductor the Under-Secretary, who drily asked me what I could expect when you are obliged to mix the sexes in this way under the same roof. What penalty is attached to detection in the demonstration of these personal attentions I do not know, but no strictness on the part of the chiefs can interdict flirtations and iced-cream at lunch-time, and no methodical arrangement of documents can prevent the young gentlemen from discovering at times that they cannot proceed with their work without consulting some paper or other which is only to be found in the ladies' rooms. No wonder that Chase and Fessenden should have collapsed under such trying circumstances. The fabrication of the notorious greenbacks was sealed to us, but we did not eat our hearts on that account, for we had seen enough of them already, and, besides, the young ladies were vastly more interesting.

We had made the acquaintance of the Washington editor of the 'New York Times'—a clever, hard-

headed Scotchman, sufficiently amusing and sarcastic
to converse with, and a perfect diplomatist to deal with.
On the whole, we did not get on very well with our
friend the editor. He was far too much like a leading
article: he talked like a leading article, he thought
like a leading article, he looked like a leading article.
His sentences were always rounded off with stops and
rests complete, pointed with some stock simile, or mystified with oracular nicety that bore any interpretation
he chose to put upon it. He made abundant profes-
sions of his readiness and ability to do for us anything
we wanted—the chief desire we had being a visit to
the army; and as he had long been a correspondent
on the field, we thought that this was in his power,
but if it was, he did not and never intended to exercise it in our favour. He hated Englishmen, and what
he called their "sublime insular indifference," with a
deadly hate, of Scotch and Yankee jealousy combined;
and consequently we did not get much out of our friend
the diplomatic editor. However, he did one thing for
us—he took us to the White House.

It is a moderately sized building of white marble,
standing a few yards back from one of the chief
avenues, and approached by the ordinary semicircular
drive of a detached villa. We were not a little surprised to find that the President's house was totally
unguarded—not even a house-dog on the watch; but
what was our astonishment to see the editor fling open

the glass swing-door, where there was not a vestige of
a porter's calves, pass through the hall, in which there
was not a soul to be seen, up the staircase, which a
domestic was cleaning (for it was yet early, and the
President had not arrived from his summer residence
outside the city), and into the President's private study.
We followed in mute amazement, half-ashamed of
treading unasked on this sacred ground; but the editor
quieted our apprehensions by assuring us that it was
all perfectly public; the people paid for this house, and
they had a right to see the inside of it; they paid the
President to live there, and they had a right to see
him in it. It was a shock to our "insular" notions,
but not the first time that they had been shocked by
this forced publicity of a man's every thought, word,
and deed. No American can have such a thing to
retire into as a *sanctum*, if he would. No American's
house is his castle, and least of all is the President's
house his castle—it is not even his house. Well,
the President's house, so far as we saw it, was furnished in the ordinary way of a private residence—
simple and unpretending in the extreme. State is so
utterly abhorred by a Yankee, that, in his desire to
avoid it, he descends to the lowest depths of meager
baldness and simplicity. He abolishes liveries, and
gowns, and wigs; he eschews crests and armorial
bearings; he abjures all the outward marks of deference and respect which we are accustomed to pay to

our superiors. But the Yankee has no superiors; the President is the people's servant. That, at any rate, is the Yankee's theory, though it may not seem just now to accord with the President's practice.

Well, I dare say you do not agree with this great levelling theory of equality. Never mind; the present President is quite contented with his lot. If you had only been with us that morning upon the steps of the White House, where we waited, with one or two more loungers like ourselves, to see the President come in from his country house, and had noticed the affectation of asceticism which characterises his goings out and comings in, you would have observed in its most extravagant form the practical result of the principles of this model republic. The President's carriage was escorted by a troop of men on horses—I cannot call them cavalry, nor mounted rifles, nor *gendarmes*, nor anything else. The animals on which they rode had four legs, and an odd tail or two, and more or less the shape and manner of a horse, and I suppose they were intended for horses; but such a lot of bow-legged, cow-quartered, dead-alive quadrupeds I never saw; I do not believe the vivisectionists of Paris would have condescended to operate upon any one of them. Of the riders themselves I can say less. They were dressed in the uniform of the Invalid Corps, light-blue, veritable shoddy, mud-bespattered, and threadbare as an Irishman's coat; such an ill-conditioned set of ruffians as Falstaff never

15

would have led through Coventry. But the escort was
worthy of its charge. It was a very dirty, tumble-
down machine, with an enormous hood, looking like a
bathing-machine with the awning out. The harness
was of the shadiest character; the horse matched the
harness, and the coachman's coat matched both, while
his hat for seediness eclipsed all—no decayed cabby
would have put his head in it. Whether it was the
traditional travelling carriage of the American Presi-
dents, or Mr. Lincoln's family coach, I did not hear.
It might have been centuries since it was washed or
painted; and grooming the horse had none; and as for
the coachman's hat, if it had not been too ancient, I
should have guessed it to be George Washington's.
The constitution has some queer provisions; I wonder
whether it compels the President's coachman to brush
his hat the wrong way. However, there was not much
to choose between the escort, the vehicle, and the
coachman—it was a disreputable turn-out altogether.
I am quite sure it would never have been allowed to
pass the gates of Hyde Park; I even doubt whether
the *sergents de ville* would have admitted it into the
Bois de Boulogne.

As the imposing *cortége* drew up at the entrance to
the house, there rose from the depths of the bathing-
machine's hood a long, lank, lath-like, darkly-clad
figure that seemed to unfold itself like the Genie of
old before the gaze of the astonished fisherman, as if

it were never coming to an end. But we watched patiently and at last the end came—and such an end. Such a pair of terminations were planted upon the pavement as could belong to no biped but a Western Yankee or a Dodo. Abe—I speak as an American citizen; and is not our evergreen premier known to us familiarly as "Pam"?—Abe, I say, had received a telegram, or had something to communicate to Stanton, so, as soon as he had got himself erect upon the pathway, he wheeled round and marched off to the War Office, very much to the disappointment of those who were thus deprived of a fair stare at him. But so far as I could then see, he did not look particularly worn or worried by the fearful weight of care upon his shoulders. He was very sallow, but all Yankees are; very ugly, and awkward, and ungainly, but that I was prepared for. He was dressed in the orthodox black in which every American citizen considers it incumbent to appear in public,—I should not wonder if it is required by the constitution—black " vest " (Anglicé waistcoat), and black " pants " (Anglicé trousers), the former velvet, and the latter "shorts;" and being a Yankee he was shod in square-toed Wellingtons, each of which, after the fashion of a true Westerner, was a *Wellingtonia gigantea*. But the President was soon out of sight, and as I had a subsequent opportunity of making a closer acquaintance with him, I will leave what more I have to say about him till I come to that occasion.

The great object on which we had set our hearts was a visit to the army of the Potomac, and to this end, armed with a letter of introduction from Mr. Macdonald, I sought an interview with Mr. Seward. The best time to see him was, I was told, the evening; so at 8 o'clock I called at his private residence. The gentleman (I suppose I cannot say "servant") who opened the door told me he was up stairs.

"May I come in?" said I.

"Guess you may."

"When can I see him?"

"Right away; first door fronting you, top of stair-case."

"Am I to go up?" said I, rather astonished at the off-hand manner of my unceremonious friend, who was retreating down the passage without so much as an offer to usher me into the presence of the great man.

"Guess so, walk right in."

I did so, though my instinctive habits led me to knock at the door before entering, a piece of delicacy which was, I find, quite superfluous, and there, in slippers and an easy chair, engaged upon the Illustrated London News, I found the secretary of state. I explained who I was, produced my letter, and was cordially welcomed.

Like his chief antagonist, Little John, Mr. Seward is of diminutive stature, not nearly so long as his despatches, but every bit as difficult to deal with.

Americans, as a rule, are so free and easy that a stranger is at home with them in a minute, but the secretary is not one of these. He was civil, and courteous, and affable, but at the same time unpleasant. One of those men who wait with a smile upon their cheeks till you have finished your sentence, and then sit upon you like a 'Saturday Review.' I talked with him a long time, asked him a great many questions without expecting a direct answer, and listened in admiration to his diplomatical replies. He talked of the English and their constitution, and explained how his was modelled on ours, with a view to the nearest approximation to constitutional perfection. He spoke of the war, of which he admitted that no one could yet see the end ; of slavery, and the difficulty of the problem ; of the coming election, which he considered no longer doubtful ; of the " Anglo-rebel " privateers, and the French occupation of Mexico. He was properly bitter about the English sympathy with the South, and said that no English paper he had seen had the slightest notion of the question at issue. He had written pages and pages to the British government to try and make them understand the war, but they were childish or obstinate, or both, and he supposed it would be left to the next generation to reveal the truth in its proper light. Having sufficiently disturbed his equilibrium by getting him on this tender point, I thought it time to go, and retired, but before leaving I got a promise from him to write to Stanton, of whom he was evidently in great alarm, for a pass for myself and companions. He did not commit himself so far as to say he thought it at all certain that we should be allowed to go to the front, which he explained was a matter of the greatest favour.

I paid several subsequent visits to the secretary of state, and found him on each occasion more oblique and diplomatic than ever. He wrote, however, according to his promise, but our desired visit to the army caused us an enormous amount of trouble, and only led us to see that red tape and circumlocution are as rampant in Washington as they are in Downing Street or Pall Mall. For ten days we persisted in our attempt, attacked everybody whom we thought in any way likely to facilitate our object, from the British ministers to the porters at the war office; colonels, captains, provost marshals, military agents, war-office clerks, secretaries, and officers of the sanitary commission; but, alas, all to no purpose. On the tenth day of our labours, just as we were on the eve of accomplishing our object, we were informed that Grant, for some reason best known to himself, probably a disaster which he did not want recorded, refused to give the required pass; and so Seward and we were snubbed. It was a bitter disappointment to us. We had wasted valuable time in Washington and done little else but " loaf" since our arrival. All that is to be seen there might have been dawdled through in a couple of days. The failure of our scheme, I am afraid, has somewhat embittered my thoughts and words about the place, but I was intensely disgusted at being kept kicking my heels there, when my time was so short, and then having to "make tracks" ἄπρακτος.

But, after all, we were not very idle, and how we amused ourselves you shall hear. Washington is now under the thumb of certain military dictators who call themselves provost-marshals, and their rod, I confess, is of particularly hard metal. No one is allowed to sojourn in the city without some satisfactory ground. No one in uniform can show in the street without a properly countersigned pass, for every quarter of the city is paraded day and night by strong patrols, by whom each passenger or lounger is stopped and called upon to produce his papers; and woe to the luckless wight whose documents are pronounced fishy. It is wonderful to see the complacence with which a Federal soldier will, for the hundredth time in one afternoon, dive into his pocket for the papers that he has already exhibited to ninety-nine corporals and their pickets; wonderful, indeed, to see the dove-like simplicity with which the American Bird o' Freedom submits to be clipped and caged. But times like these must have their Syllas, and I do not suppose the despotism of the North can compare in tyranny with that of Richmond. We are not inconvenienced by it beyond the

nuisance of being confined to the streets and suburbs
without the possibility of getting outside; at least,
unless provided with the requisite pass. I made two
or three attempts at the bridges across the Potomac,
but was always received with half a dozen bayonets,
and ordered back into the city; and as the rifles
were all loaded, I thought it imprudent to make a
bolt of it and give the sentries a running shot.
However, finding that we had so much time on our
hands, and being tired of being boxed up in the city,
we sought the editor of the *New York Times*, and
with the help of his department, and my letter to
Seward, added to natural advantages of a general mild-
ness about our looks and language, and one or two
" white lies," we got a pass from the provost-marshal,
and a hearty shake of the hand, and after putting our
names to a declaration of secresy as to what we should
see and hear, we were allowed to leave the charmed
circle.

It was a pleasant triumph at the bridge to be challenged by the fiery sentries, and squash them with the
production of the magic talisman from the provost-
marshal's. They grounded arms and were civil. We
crossed the long bridge that spans the Potomac, passed
through the earthworks and stockade with which its
southern gate is defended, and stood in Virginia. But
do not expect me to " gush " about the thoughts that
rushed to my brain upon first setting foot in Rebeldom.

The only sensation I remember to have experienced at that moment was much lower in order and position, traceable in a great degree, I suspect, to immoderate excesses in peaches and ice-creams. Our first object was Arlington House, the home of General Lee; but on the way we visited a negro settlement called Freedman's Village. It lies upon a high airy bluff overlooking the Potomac just within the Federal lines, and has been established by the Federal Government as an asylum for fugitive or captured slaves. Several thousands are now in the settlement, which is composed of a number of streets of log huts, all clean and neat as model lodging houses. The men are taught different trades, the women needlework, and the children are well schooled. As we came up to the school the little blacks were coming out to play, the very picture of fun and merriment, as full of playfulness as kittens, as boisterous in their ebullitions of it as English school children in their happiest humour; such a contrast from the Yankee school-child, who has not a spark of the kitten in him, who hates toys and games and boyishness, and talks Wall Street shop before he is in his teens. It would have done you good to see these little imps tumbling about in their gambols. They were the queerest little creatures in the world, all hues and shapes and sizes; several of them with hair of the brightest yellow, as if they had been dipped head-first in a paint-pot; some of them all head, like tadpoles;

others all belly, like chimpanzees. I spoke to the
schoolmaster, and asked him whether he had any
difficulty .in teaching them.   His answer was, "Less
difficulty than he had often had with whites."   What
a practical refutation of all the Huxleyite bosh which
has been talked of late at the Anthropological!   Any
one who watches the niggers that wait at table in the
Yankee hotels cannot fail to see a marked difference
of character between them and white-skinned waiters ;
a childishness about their actions, a stolid apathy in
their looks and movements, which indicate the absence
of intellectual education.   But, after all, they seem to
me a good bit brighter than many a clodhopper I have
known at home, and I have not the slightest doubt
that the clodhopper is none the worse for being free,
nor the least faith in the good conscience of those who
deny the negro any mental capacity beyond that of an
ourang-outang.   Ages of ignorance and oppression
have smothered the intellectual fire, but it burns yet
amongst the embers, and who shall say that it cannot
be vivified ?   Freedman's Village is a good work, the
only pity is that there is not more of it.

Four miles from Washington we found ourselves at
Arlington House, standing at the open window of the
dining room and looking back across the Potomac at
the glorious view of the distant city.   The house is
placed in a lovely situation on the crest of a beautifully wooded slope.   It is a queer old-fashioned place,

with heavy columns and flights of steps, strangely like what it is being now turned into—a mausoleum. The doors were all wide open, and we walked in unquestioned by the soldiers who were lounging about the entrance. The rooms had been sacked of their best furniture and looked dreary and desolate. A few pictures remained upon the walls, one or two of them apparently of merit, which chance had saved from the bayonet for the Federal Government, who were going to put them up for sale. The carpets and curtains had gone; a few tables and chairs alone were left for the use of the soldiers who occupied the building. In front workmen were busy restoring the outer wall, for the park has been enclosed as a cemetery, and the house is to be the mausoleum. As we came into the park we had stopped to turn into a burial ground, where the victims of one night's assault had been laid to their last rest. The graves were in long parallelograms, divided by narrow lanes, each grave so close to its neighbour that the bodies must have all but touched. The Federal gravestones were marked with the names and regiments of those at whose heads they stood. The enemy's, which were promiscuously interspersed with them, were delineated with the single word REBEL. I cannot say how many hundreds there were, but I know that as I stood amongst them I was as much moved as if they had been as many thousands. Here was the result of a single assault upon the ranks of one brigade. Heaven knows how many other spirits fled to their home that night. It was one of the saddest sights I have ever seen. None of the crippled forms I had seen in the streets, none of the bleeding wounds that I had met with in the cars, not even the ghastly look of a poor fellow whose leg had just been summarily amputated at a railway station, turned me so sick and sorrowful as the sight of that soldiers' burial ground. And then to see the home of Robert Lee sacked and made into a cemetery, and to fancy the thoughts that would fill that great heart to behold the work of devastation going on, and to feel oneself actually in the presence of war with all its attendant horrors, and in the midst of people blinded to them by the blunting experience of four years' bloodshed. All these thoughts, and others like them, were so strange to me, and in their strangeness so painful, that I doubt whether I ever had a sadder walk than that visit to the heights of Arlington.

From Arlington House we made our way across the rough uneven ground of which the southern bank of the river consists to some of the outlying forts that form the defences of Washington. I shall not say much about them; not that I consider that anything my inexperienced pen might reveal could give such information to any one as would violate my oath of secrecy; but because I really know so little about fortifications that I cannot undertake to make them interesting. All I can say is that to me the place looked quite impregnable. I never found any position in which I could stand without being exposed to a cross fire from at least three batteries. I never saw one battery that was not commanded by half a dozen others. Every fort was in the orthodox star shape, with ditch and drawbridge and bomb-proof barracks; internally a model of engineering skill, and externally a tangled mass of pointed stakes and awkward trees with their branches all turned outwards and sharpened like needles, and black muzzles peering through them; and beyond all was a long line of rifle pits enclosing the whole of the fortifications, which cover an extent of ground that is incredible; and if this is the sort of thing that has to be confronted before Richmond, and they tell me the works there are much stronger, I do not see, for my part, why the place should not hold out for ever. From these heights, and from those of George Town, which we afterwards ascended, upon the opposite bank, the views of Washington were magnificent. The lofty white dome of the Capitol rising out of the dense foliage of its gardens, and towering above the low buildings of the city is always a beautiful object in the distance; the basin in which the city lies, the Potomac and its lovely banks, the Italian skies and clear horizon, are worthy of the pen of a Ruskin or the pencil of a Turner; but distance is everything with Washington, and when you are once inside the outskirts the sweet illusion is gone like a dream.

I suppose you want to hear something of my impressions of the army. Well, to my mind, the Federal soldier is very much like the English militiaman, only that his hair and his legs are longer, his uniform is dirtier, and his whole cut more unmilitary. The dress is blue, Cambridge blue trousers and Oxford blue coat. The officers, many of them in entire suits of dark blue, look very much like our officers of the Royal Navy, except that they have no epaulettes. Indeed there is little or no ornament on the dress. The grades are marked by plain gilt bars upon the collar or the wrist or shoulder, and occasionally something extra upon the cap. This is generally the French cut foraging cap, with its diminutive crown; but some regiments wear a tasty black brigand's hat, with a gold cord and tassel round it, that looks spicy and picturesque, and this hat is even sported to a great extent by other regiments when swelling it about off duty. But the Federal uniform is not at all showy or attractive, and if I did not know what a fascination there is in any toggery, however unsightly, which is designed for military purposes, I should think it marvellous that the Federal officers should be so fond of their uniforms; but when the 31st Surrey Volunteers see nothing unbecoming in their dress, why should the Yankee captain be ashamed of his? The invalid corps, which forms a sort of household guard, is completely arrayed in the most radical of blues, and looks for all the world exactly like the sky-blue band of the C. U. V. C. I seemed to see a Sippel in every one of them.

As for the men themselves, they are undoubtedly a goodly medley. Lanky, rawboned, scraggy, and angular, all who are Yankee; short and wiry, those who are Irish or French; round and podgy, such as are Germans. I do not see that the foreigners are in any large proportion; and if they were, why should it not be so, considering the enormous numbers of alien immigrants who have been annually peopling the country, and reaping the advantages, whatever they may be, of the Government under which they have chosen to put themselves? If there is any benefit to be derived from Republican Constitutions, why should not those who attach themselves to them take up arms in their defence? And, looking at it in this light, the foreign element seems to me by no means largely represented in the ranks. But I daresay you will not listen to me on this point in opposition to the ' Times,' so I will leave you to read it when the history of the war shall be impartially written, and pass on. I mentioned that the men I saw of Sherman's army were remarkably fine fellows—we shall hear more of them before the war is over—but Grant's army is of evidently much inferior material. However, they are not to be despised, I can assure you. They are not very perfect in their step, or their movements, or their manual exercise; they are not very strictly disciplined, and if a man is told to shoulder arms, and wants to blow his nose he will, as I heard one tell his captain that he "will do it presently." But their organization is well adapted for the country in which they have to fight. As skirmishers, I believe, they are excellent. Thoroughly imbued with the American theory of self-help and independence, each man feels himself an important unit in his corps, does battle on his own hook without prompting, and in the wild wooded battle-fields of this continent such tactics are indispensable. The behaviour of the troops in the town is most exemplary. Notwithstanding the presence in the streets and suburbs of 60,000 to 70,000 men, the thoroughfares are as orderly as Belgrave Square. But then the pickets are numerous, and the Provost Marshal's wrath inexorable. But if you want to see a queer sight, come and look at a negro regiment. Niggers anyhow are ungainly, and niggers in uniform are *not* soldier-like; but I must say they do not drill badly. In fact they are so habituated to submission that immediate obedience to orders comes natural to them, and more than one captain has told me that he would far sooner command a company of blacks than whites. It is difficult to get at the truth about their efficiency on the field, but in numerical strength alone they must be very formidable. Their capability for military service has been proved, and it seems to me that they will hereafter form a valuable and convenient weapon to use against any foreign power. For the cavalry that I saw I cannot say much. Their animals looked like superannuated cab-horses: their equestrian attainments were most elementary; they were always bespattered with mud, uncivilised and unwholesome.

You cannot be half an hour in the streets of Washington now without seeing a detachment of deserters being again marched off to the front; for desertion, technically "bounty-jumping," has now become a regular trade, and men have been known to "jump" the bounty and "start off" as many as twenty times. I cannot understand why the Government does not execute summary vengeance upon such rascals, but the only punishment they meet with when caught is to be forwarded to the front, and there, of course, in a country of this extent, they slip off again with the greatest ease. If you do not see any Federal deserters you will see a gang of Confederate prisoners under escort to the rear. I saw lots of them being marched past the door of my hotel. They were always devoid of any uniform, clad in garments of every cut and hue, sometimes coatless, sometimes hatless, sometimes even with naked feet. What a picture of privation and misery! Many of them were fine handsome fellows, some of them old and gray-headed, some almost children.

16

Terse and true words those of Grant's, that to fill their ranks the Confederate Government had "robbed the cradle and the grave." But the bravery of these men is undisputed. Loudest of all in their praises have been the Federal soldiers with whom I have conversed: it reflects favorably upon themselves to tell them, but the tales they have told me of individual heroism are astonishing.

The Arsenal claimed our attention for a short while. Like that at Boston, and any other that has been established in the Northern States, it was a scene of endless bustle and activity. Parrotts, and Armstrongs, and Whitworths were being finally adjusted upon their carriages; Enfield and a hundred other sorts of muskets being finished for use; shot being cast, and shell filled; ambulances in course of manufacture, and ammunition in preparation for the front. It really is wonderful to see the gigantic scale upon which all these operations are being carried on—the miles of workshops that have been erected—the acres of ground that are covered with the deadly apparatus of war—the multitude of the armed hosts of these modern Xerxes'—the fleets of these baby Nelsons; and to think that barely four years back they had hardly a gun or hand to use one. Dogs are provided by nature with the ready implements of warfare, and therefore their delight in biting is instinctive; but truly fighting seems to come as naturally to human kind. However, I do

not think the Americans are by choice a military nation.   They will bark as loud as you like, but biting
is not their pastime ; and I have little doubt that when
the end of this war comes they will find it much more
congenial to their nature to retire peaceably to their
stores and offices than to turn out to fight a foreign
foe.

There is one other institution of the day of which
I must say a few words, and that is the Sanitary
Commission.   We had a letter of introduction to the
secretary, and by his kindness were enabled to learn
something of the working of this somewhat anomalous
establishment.   I say anomalous, because I think the
peculiarity of the institution must strike any one from
the Old World even more forcibly than the gigantic
scale on which it works.   It seemed to me so extraordinary to find a volunteer association like this co-
existing and co-operating with the Government in the
administration of those departments wherein we ordi-
narily see the executive vested in the Government as
their absolute prerogative—to see citizens, men and
women, without any other warrant than their patriotism, exercising surveillance over the conduct of the
State in that very one of its functions which it usually
most jealously guards against intrusion—the organization of the national forces.   After that terrible Crimean
winter in which our troops rotted away like sheep,
till they lost one half of their effective force, our

Government agreed to the appointment of a Sanitary
Commission to save the remnant of the army; but that
Commission had to confine itself to the reorganization
of the medical department and the recommendation of
hygienic precautions.　But the United States' Sanitary Commission goes far beyond that.　Organized
originally to secure the greater health and comfort of
the troops, it has gradually assumed to itself a hundred
collateral duties, till now, after planting its civilian
agents, doctors, inspectors, in the midst of every camp,
it has charged itself with the duty, not only of taking
care of the sick and wounded, but of making army
censuses, obtaining transport for the soldiers, both to
the field and home again, examining the cause of
punishments inflicted, and obtaining redress where
equitable, providing pay and pensions; in fact, defending the interests of the troops, not only against rogues
and speculators, but even, in case of need, against the
Government itself.　The secretary said, and I think
justly, that such an organization as this could have no
existence in any country but America.　It is essen-
tially the creature of a republic; its root is the people
—a social body of individual members, born and bred
to the spirit of individual inaction, which works by
coalition and independent associations.　The conduct
of the war is entrusted to the Government, but the
people fight, and the people have a right to see that
their interests are duly cared for by the Government for

whom they fight—to supplement what the Government has omitted—to oppose what it has done wrongly. The Commission is the people's agent—their trustee, accountable to them for the due performance of the trust committed to it—the welfare of the soldier. This seems to be the theory of the institution. To you it may naturally enough appear to do little else than that which is properly the work of the War Office; but remember the circumstances under which the war burst upon the North—the absence of any efficient military organization—the inexperience of the Government in the task entrusted to it—the scale on which all had to be carried on; and you will better see the origin of the Commission, if not the justification of its enormous powers. Still, I confess that it is difficult to understand the spirit of the chiefs who will tolerate such interference with the executive.

It would be impossible, in the space of a letter, to give you any idea of the colossal work which the Commission undertakes. The honour of having given the first impulse to it belongs to the American women. Fort Sumter had hardly fallen when ladies' societies were formed in every corner of the Union to aid the patriotism of the soldiers by a devotion to their interests as patriotic. Bazaars were held, supplies collected, money poured in with munificent liberality; and the good work still continues so full and free, that the Commission has now a million dollars in its hands, and supplies more numerous than it can distribute. Every local agency, however distant, is connected with a State centre; each State central office, with one of the two grand central administrative agencies for the army of the East or West; which last are directly connected with the respective armies upon the field. The organization of the system seems wonderful. The ramification of its many branches, as depicted on the ingenious chart which the secretary has made, astonished us with its compass and simplicity. I cannot stop to tell you of half that the secretary showed us. It was a most interesting day that we spent in visiting the receiving houses where the supplies are stored, the offices where the inquiries of relatives are answered, and those where the soldiers' papers are corrected, and their wages and pensions paid; the homes where discharged and furloughed men are housed, and fed, and kept safely from the jaws of the rogues and sharpers who are ever ready to prey upon them, until they can be conveniently forwarded to their respective destinations. This last—the Special Relief service—is one of the most striking works of the Commission. It steps in with the needed advice and means of relief just where, under the rigid regulations of military rule, the army authorities leave the broken-down, furloughed, discharged, or invalided soldiers, and takes them forcibly into its safe keeping. Add to all this the provision of hospitals, soldiers' homes, hospital trains, writing ma-

terials and stamps, means of transit, and a thousand
other acts of benevolence, and, not least, the proposed
establishment of sanitaria, where maimed men are to
be taught the means of getting a livelihood by the use
of the members which the chances of war have still
left them; and you will get an inkling of the important
part which the Sanitary Commission plays in the history of the present war.

There are two notorieties of the day of whom I have
a little to say, and then I shall have done with Washington. The first is General Grant. I knew that the
general had been for several days in Willard's Hotel,
but I never was able to see him. I had asked several
people to point him out to me in the hall and reading-
rooms, but was always met with the observation that
he had that instant brushed up against me; but he
was always away and out of sight before I could get a
look at him. He haunted me like a will o'-the-wisp
that I never could come up with, till I began to think
myself the victim of a 1st of April hoax. But one
morning at breakfast I sat opposite a little chap with
an enormous appetite—a short, pug-nosed, monkey-
faced little fellow, with a close-trimmed beard, like a
quickset hedge, rather red, and very prickly; and I do
not know that I should have taken any particular notice
of him, if he had not been so silent and voracious as
he was. Coming out of the coffee-room, I asked a
waiter for the hundredth time to show me the general.

He turned and pointed to a dumpy little man then
walking towards us—no other than my little table
companion with the powerful digestion. The waiter's
revelation amazed me. The figure to whom my attention was directed was the very last amongst the hundreds in and out the hotel every day upon which I
should have pitched as being that of the General
Commander-in-chief of the army of the Potomac.
Such an unmilitary, insignificant exterior could not, I
could have wagered anything, cover the soldier-like
material of which Ulysses Grant has shown himself to
be composed. I stepped after him and took another
stare, but it only confirmed my astonishment. He
looked more like a mechanic than ever, and a very
ordinary one, too. How often it is that one's anticipations of great men are grievously disappointed by a
glimpse of the original—how the ideal picture is dashed
to atoms by the photograph! I never had my aërial
castle more thoroughly demolished than in the case of
General Grant. He may be a good horse to go, but
he is a most undoubted rum one to look at; or, as
the Yankees say, " he's a smart old 'oss, but his looks
is very small pertaters." The general was in Washington upon a consultation with the President as to
an intended attack on Richmond, in which I heard, on
good authority, that the general purposed to sacrifice the
lives of 25,000 of his men—the sum at which he set the
cost of success—as coolly and deliberately as a man might

talk of venturing a stake of twenty-five cents upon any
of the gambling-tables of New York. It is a horrible
way of doing business, and so think his officers; but
Grant believes it the cheapest way in the end, and life
in America is held cheap as dirt. But for all this cold-
blooded indifference to the value of life, and bulldog
tenacity of purpose, Grant is a popular man with those
whose lives he plays with, and for no other reason, I
believe, than that he refuses to swell about in his uniform and distinctive marks of his exalted rank; but he
has other claims upon the favour of the country, and
the people look to him as the general who is to give
the South her death-blow.

The other celebrity of whom I have a few words to
say is Mr. Lincoln. I had been very anxious to get
an introduction to him; but the summer vacation was
but half through, and he was only in Washington a
few hours every day, so that my chance of an interview
seemed small. However, as I observed before, public
life in America has no private side at all. What is an
American citizen elected to the Presidency and paid
for but to sit at home and listen at all hours to the
wants of all who choose to assail him, from the clouds
of hungry office-seekers to the country bumpkins lionising the city? So we went to our friend the Under-
Secretary of the Treasury, and told him we wanted to
see the President, and could he manage it for us? Oh,
yes! his daughter knew Abe well; she would take us

up in the evening to his country seat—the thing was as simple as possible. Accordingly, at seven o'clock one evening, I and my two fellow-travellers called in a carriage at the Under-Secretary's, and carried off his daughter with us. We had hardly seen her before, but that made no difference, and she was emphatically one of those strong-minded young ladies (and what American girl is not?) who can take care of themselves without *chaperons*, and very well, too. It was dark when we reached the President's residence, so that we could see little of what it was like, beyond the fact that it stood in a sort of park, and was guarded by a regiment of troops, encamped picturesquely about the grounds; for the house is some way beyond the Federal lines, and the neighbourhood is infested with guerillas, to whom the President's head would be worth its weight in gold. There is a hospital in the enclosure, and Stanton, the Minister of War, has a house there, too; so that there is quite a nursery of government officials under the protection of these particular bayonets.

We drove up to the door, and being challenged by the sentry, replied with becoming modesty that we wanted to see Mr. and Mrs. Lincoln. He let us pass, and we rang. I rather expected the door to have been opened by the disreputable coachman; but we were waited upon by a buttonless buttons, apparently the sole domestic on the premises, to whom we told our wish. He suggested that it was rather late for an interview with Mr. and Mrs. Lincoln, and as it was then considerably past eight, I thought the hint very reasonable. Not so the Secretary's daughter. With ready wit and admirable *aplomb*, she bade the officious page to go in and tell his master that there were three gentlemen there, who had come three thousand miles for the express purpose of seeing him and his lady, and did not intend to go away till they had done so. The message, or the way in which it was delivered, or both, frightened the page, and I suppose the President, too. Who he imagined the three distinguished visitors to be, or how much his anticipations were disappointed, I know not; but at any rate he yielded at once to the *ultimatum* of our fair companion, so far, at least, as to consent to gratify us with a sight of himself; but Mrs. Lincoln had retired to her room, and was not well enough to come down. I must confess I was very much ashamed of myself for disturbing a quiet couple in this unceremonious way; but it seemed to be all *en règle*, and if you are in Turkey, as the burlesque writers say, why not do as the Turkeys do? We were ushered into a moderate-sized, neatly furnished drawing-room, where we were told the President would see us immediately. We had sat there but a few minutes, when there entered through the folding doors the long, lanky, lath-like figure that we had seen descending from the one-horse-shay, with hair ruffled, and eyes very sleepy, and—hear it, ye votaries of court etiquette !—feet enveloped in carpet slippers.   We all rose somewhat confused by this abrupt introduction to the presence of the highest in the land, except, of course, the Secretary's daughter, who immediately offered her hand to the President, and in a few apt words explained who she was, and why she was there.   Mr. Lincoln advanced to me and my fellow-travellers, shook each of us warmly by the hand, expressed his pleasure at seeing us, and told us to take seats and make ourselves comfortable.   We did so, and were at home at once.   All my uneasiness and awe vanished in a moment before the homely greeting of the President, and the genial smile which accompanied it ; and had they not, a glance at one of the carpet slippers jogging up and down upon the knee of the other leg in the most delightful freedom of attitude, would have reassured me, were I a Nathaniel Winkle.

The conversation was briskly kept up by the President.   It began, naturally enough, with questions about our tour, and the invariable interrogation that every American puts to a stranger as to what he thinks of "our great country;" and then, after a passing allusion to the war, and a remark that we were seeing his country at an unfortunate time, Mr. Lincoln turned to England, and its political aspect and constitution ; and thence he went off, unasked, into a forcibly drawn sketch of the constitution of the United States, and the

material points of difference between the governments
of the two countries. I have frequently remarked,
since landing, the accurate knowledge possessed by
Americans upon a subject of which nine out of every
ten Englishmen are in utter ignorance. The constitution is one of the first things which is drilled into
an American child; not that it requires much drilling
to induce him to imbibe it—he takes to it instinctively
as a curate to his bread and scrape—and any one, man,
woman, or child, can give a fair exposition of the subject. We had heard several before this, and began to
get rather tired of them; but we were glad, of course,
to listen to anything upon the matter from the highest
authority in the land, especially as his commentary
was very lucid and intelligent. Of course he asked
what our trade was; and hearing that it was law, he
launched off into some shrewd remarks about the legal
systems of the two countries, and then talked of the
landed tenures of England, and said we had some
"queer things in the legal way" at home, of which he
seemed to think "quit rents" as queer as any. And
then he told us how, "in the State of Kentucky, where
he was raised, they used to be troubled with the same
mysterious relics of feudalism, and titles got into such
an almighty mess with these pettifoggin' incumbrances
turnin' up at every fresh tradin' with the land, and no
one knowin' how to get rid of 'em, as this here airth
never saw;" and how he managed to relieve the titles,

and made his first step to fame in doing so. It was a treat to hear him talk of his early life, with a certain quiet pride in his rise from the bottom of the ladder. And why is it not a matter to be proud of ? and where is the sting of the jeers of our English journals against the humble origin of Lincoln, the " rail-splitter?" Abraham Lincoln has enemies enough, Heaven knows ; but " he never makes a friend that never makes a foe ;" and I am quite convinced that the President has many excellent qualities, which will some day or other be recognised and appreciated. As for the stories in circulation about his tyranny and heartlessness, I do not believe a word of them. Just look at his physiognomy; it is not beautiful—Mrs. Lincoln herself could not make it so; but at any rate you will see a winning smile in his eye, which, if nothing else can, will give the lie to such calumnies. But sit and talk with him for an hour, and note the instinctive kindliness of his every thought and word, and say if you have ever known a warmer-hearted, nobler spirit.

The conversation next turned upon English poetry, the President saying that when we disturbed him he was deep in Pope. He seemed to be a great admirer of Pope, especially of his " Essay on Man ; " going so far as to say that he thought it contained all the religious instruction which it was necessary for a man to know. Then he mused for a moment or two, and asked us if we could show him any finer lines

than those ending, as he quoted them without hesi-
tation—

> " All nature is but art, unknown to thee ;
> All chance, direction, which thou canst not see ;
> All discord, harmony not understood ;
> All partial evil, universal good :
> And, spite of pride, in erring treason's spite,
> One truth is clear, whatever is, is right."

And here, on getting to the last few words, his instinctive humour broke out, for to an extremely flat
remark of mine upon the beauty of the verses he had
repeated, he replied with a smile—

" Yes, that's a convenient line, too, that last one.
You see, a man may turn it, and say, ' Well, if whatever *is* is right, why, then, whatever *isn't* must be
wrong.' "

And then he went off into a broad laugh, and we
laughed, too—not so much at the joke, which we
thought decidedly poor, as at the way in which he
delivered himself of it. The laugh ended, and I rose
to go. I had heard the President make a joke—a
very mild one, it is true—but I felt that the second
great object of my visit to the country (Niagara being
my first) had been achieved, and my mission, so to
speak, was accomplished. The Secretary's daughter,
after another hint at her regret that we could not have
the chance of seeing Mrs. Lincoln—to which the President replied, " I guess we shall not get to see Mrs.

Lincoln down here again to-night"—rose and thanked him for his courtesy in according us so pleasant an interview; and the President, in return, assured her and us that the meeting had been equally agreeable to himself; and thanking us cordially for coming to see him, gave us each a hearty grip of the hand—it was much more than a shake—and we withdrew. So ended our visit to the President, a much more pleasant one than I ever had with any other potentate; and here shall end my talk of Washington, for I fear that I must have wearied you with details enough, though perhaps you may be willing to excuse them as a simple record of an evening with one of the great historical characters of this century.

XI.

PHILADELPHIA AND NEW YORK.

LONDON ;
Christmas, 1864.

THERE still remain two of the most important cities of the Union of which I have had no time to say a word, Philadelphia and New York ; and yet they would each have afforded material for an ample letter.   I shall not now trouble you at any length with either of them, but simply give you a few extracts from a diary made upon the spot.   And first of Philadelphia, whither we proceeded direct from Washington.   Of all the cities of the American continent which I visited, I think Philadelphia pleased me most.   In grandeur of street-architecture the Quaker City is unsurpassed, as a whole, by New York ; in cleanliness it is unrivalled, I should imagine, by any city in the world.   I do not suppose any Dutch village could match in purity its great thoroughfares.   A speck of dirt upon the snow-white pavements of Philadelphia would cause as much uneasiness as a chalk-mark on a sweep's nose.   The buff-bricked houses, with their green blinds, looked to

17

me as if they had just come out of a bath. The paint
was everywhere as fresh and bright as if it had been
laid on yesterday. Of the streets themselves I need
tell you little; they are, like those of every other city
of the continent I saw but Boston, straight as the
furrows of a well-ploughed field; but unlike Chicago,
and Buffalo, and Detroit, and Washington, less wide
and straggling, and so, in my opinion, more handsome.
The lions to be seen are the Hall of Independence,
where the famous Declaration was signed—a grand
piece of composition, by the bye, with which I wonder
the University professionals do not experimentalise, in
preference to many specimens of classical English which
they operate upon for Greek or Latin prose. The
pride which the Americans take in lionising a Britisher
over the hall is thoroughly characteristic of the people.
I suppose I was questioned a hundred times about it
by various parties who wished to get a rise out of me.
Had I seen it? When should I see it? Should I
mind seeing it? Surely I should not leave the continent without a look at the arm-chair? Did I notice
the ink-stand and the pen? Well, I *have* seen it, and
I do not think much of it. It is a dingy old room,
unworthy of the name of hall, extremely dirty, and not
particularly well cared-for. However, it is one of the
few historical antiquities that the Americans have to
show, and, as such, it was of great interest. But I
must say I thought the view from the summit of the

steeple above the hall much the best part of the show.
—Next amongst the lions are the park and the water-
works. These works are constructed upon the Delaware for the supply of the city. The water from the
river is forced up by a mill, worked by the natural fall
of the stream into enormous reservoirs many feet above
the banks. The works themselves are on a tremendous
scale; but we in this country can show the same sort
of undertakings on a scale, I dare say, far more magnificent. However, I doubt if the English people have
the same faculty that the Americans possess of com-
bining ornament with utility. It would be impossible
to conceive anything more tasty and elegant than the
manner in which the slopes and vicinity of the reservoirs are converted into ornamental gardens, which
have become the fashionable promenade of the citizens.
The scenery of the Delaware at the spot in question is
most beautiful: lofty banks, covered with fine timber,
pretty villas peering through the foliage, lovely walks
upon the wooded slopes, have given the Philadelphians
an opportunity for a public park which is justly called
by them unique.

Close by is another lion—the Girard College—
a white marble edifice, in the style of a Greek temple,
with noble columns, like those of the Parthenon,
and handsome steps leading up to them. The college, which is designed for poor orphans, was shown us
by one of the masters; and we were much asto-

nished by the excellent system of education which is pursued within its walls. The children are taught various trades—not only the practical work, but the theory of the thing as well. A lecture on electricity was being delivered to them when we were there, illustrated by the most perfect instruments that I have ever known in the possession of a school. In fact, so far as I have seen or heard anything of the general education of the people, it is quite evident to me that the Americans are far in advance of us. You have only to talk for five minutes to the first person you meet in the street—a common labourer, if you like—to find out that they have solved a question which is puzzling the brains of our legislators to little or no purpose. For my own part, I can see little force in the application to the educational question of the argument that no one values what is freely given to him so much as that which he has to pay for. The axiom may be often true enough; but this matter concerns the children rather than the parents; and it seems to me a cruel answer to give to those immediately concerned, that a free education is to be withheld from them because, forsooth, their parents would not appreciate it; and so the child is to have no teaching unless the parent is able to pay the sum which is supposed necessary to secure its due appreciation. The free-schools of America diffuse throughout the Union an amount of popular education which I do not believe we shall ever arrive at until we follow a similar system. There a child from the lowest ranks of life may be trained and fitted for the highest without the expenditure on his education of a single farthing; school-books even are found him gratis. From the infant or primary school he passes on to the second school; from that, if worthy, he is transferred to the third stage—the academy—whence he is turned out into the world with a store of practical knowledge which eminently fits him for commercial life; and all gratis, and therefore, I suppose, unappreciated! Go to the States, and see for yourself. Talk with the people, and hear their wonderful amount of what we call "general information;" look at their libraries, their reading-rooms, their cheap literature, the extraordinary number of their daily journals, their love of reading for reading's sake. See, too, their admiration of the highest styles of English authorship; their fondness of Shakespeare, whom I really think some of them believe to have been an American; their love of Tennyson, whose last poem, which I bought at Chicago, has had almost as extensive a sale in America as it has had at home. Read the report of the Schools Commissioners, and see the evidence of the scientific men examined by them, to the effect that geological and such-like works find a readier sale in the States of the Union than they do in this country. And then say if you think the Americans fail to appreciate the advantages of education. But the subject is too comprehensive for a hasty letter, and I must tell you something more of Philadelphia.

It was election time in the State of Pennsylvania. The State officers were to be elected the day after I arrived, and this, the first of the State elections, was looked forward to with intense interest by the whole Union as an indication of the ultimate result of the coming Presidential election. Pennsylvania's vote— "the key-stone State"—has generally decided the final judgment of the other States; and so the excitement was quite sensational to see which party she would return as her representative, the Democrats or the Republicans. I do not think the Republicans had much apprehension about their ultimate success; but in the city itself the Democrat party was known to be very strong, and the contest likely to be severe. The streets, of course, were very gay. Americans are always hanging out flags; and by the time I reached Philadelphia, I suppose I had seen a greater quantity of floating canvas than I had seen in the course of my whole life. But all the banners that had met my eye in the course of my travel across the States were nothing as compared with the endless display which that day waved from mast and pole in the streets of Philadelphia. Over the roof of every hotel, and above the smokeless chimneys of the houses, out of the windows of the tall marble warehouses, and over the doorways of the stores, fluttered, in every size and shape, the

everlasting stars and stripes. You cannot imagine the
native partiality of a Yankee for the abstract theory of
a flag. I assure you that I have grown so weary of
the practical results of this monomania that I began
at one time to see stars and stripes in everything I
turned my eyes to. The sale of flags must be enormous. The war has put them at a premium; and not
banners only, and pennants, and standards; for the
shop-windows blaze with the national emblem printed
and woven in stuffs of every kind that can be converted
into handkerchiefs, shirts, cuffs, or collars. If the
men ever wore any nether garments but the eternal
" sabbaticals," which they do not, I have no doubt I
should have seen the stars and stripes floating round
their spindle calves, or tucked into their Wellingtons.
If the women ever condescended to wear anything half
so quiet, which they do not, I should have expected
to see their bonnets and dresses starred and striped
like their handkerchiefs. But stars and stripes even
are not enough for Philadelphia on her election-days.
She breaks out in a perfect flag fever; and so, besides
all the national banners that wave by hundreds from
each side of the streets, she strings across every thoroughfare, above the heads of the car and carriage
drivers, whole acres of variegated stuffs blazoned with
all the electioneering symbols that the sign-fabricators
can concoct—portraits of the rival candidates, treated
with unmistakable partiality by heavily biassed pencils;

short biographies, and characteristic sayings of the
various competitors, compiled by commentators more
partial still; deifications of their own man, and libel-
lous calumniations of the foe; terse condensations of
the principles and tenets of the two parties, and the
arguments for supporting this or that. You might
walk for hours up and down the streets with the back
edge of your collar in the nape of your neck, scanning
and reading the endless roll of pictures, mottoes, senti-
ments, and sensation that flaunts across the centre of
the road.   Have you ever been in Genoa?   If you
have you will recollect how in that wonderful city of
extremes of new and old, good and bad, grand palaces
and filthy alleys, side by side in harmonious discord,
there is invariably to be seen fluttering from the windows something that adds to the inexhaustible supply
of colour—sometimes, perhaps, a curtain, sometimes a
bed, sometimes a carpet, sometimes a line-full of tattered clothes, a string of the brightest, gaudiest hues
—always something exquisitely out of place and artis-
tically picturesque.   I do not mean to say that Philadelphia is in the smallest way like Genoa.   Perhaps
there are no two cities in the world more unlike. You
might drop a pin's head on the snow-white pavements
of Philadelphia and find it as easily as your glove;
you might almost drop your glove in Genoa and lose
it as readily as a pin's head.   But I must say that the
aspect of the Quaker City brought back to me most

vividly the lights and colours of old Genoa, only that
it was much more like Greenwich fair, save that it was
far too respectable.

The streets, you will gather then, were gay enough,
and the people, too, were all astir. Lincoln and
M'Clellan badges were sported like dolls on the Derby
day. Knots of loungers were talking earnestly on the
side-walks, eager faces were hurrying to and fro; but
where was the row? My only idea of an election was
the hustings, which I soon found the Americans did
not keep; and not being able to make them understand
what I wanted to see I naturally enough, as I thought,
asked to be shown the place where "all the row" was.
They laughed, and said I should not find any. What,
universal suffrages, ballot-boxes, Baines and Berkeley,
and no row? I repeat it, none whatever. The votes
were taken at certain houses fitted up for the occasion
distributed throughout the different wards of the city,
whither the electors repair to vote, and these polling
places are known as "precincts." By the precincts
stand a few men with a number of small bundles of
paper slips neatly tied up with a piece of thread, on
which are printed the names of the several candidates
for the offices that are to be filled up. These are the
voting papers or tickets. Each party has its ticket
distributors, who take care that every one shall be
duly presented with a proper bundle. The electors
instinctively form themselves into a *queue*, and advance

in order to the window at which the votes are taken, and there they deposit in the box one or other of the two tickets, republican or democratic, as their taste and fancy lead them. This done they move off as quietly and orderly as if they were in church. No speechifying, no hooting, no peelers and rotten eggs. Well, I thought, if this was the result of voting by ballot, it was the tamest thing imaginable, and if I never opposed it for any other reason I certainly should object to it as the death-blow of all the fun that is to be got out of an election.

But my hopes of some excitement were not entirely blighted. The day passed off mildly enough, but when the business was done, and the results were made known, I began to see that the true Anglo Saxon mob element was not altogether extinct. The head-quarters of the two parties were established opposite to one another in the main street, and there, as the evening came on, there congregated a crowd as noisy and boisterous as any British elector could wish to see. By ten o'clock the results of the voting in the various wards were coming in fast and ominous, and as they arrived they were posted up in a transparency, for no Stentor's lungs could have conveyed them intelligibly to the noisy throng below. The night drew on, and the excitement increased. Each fresh announcement of the state of the poll was hailed with louder cheers and hisses than the last; and then, about eleven o'clock, the streets were besieged by processions of representatives of the different wards, bearing before them in a transparency their respective numbers, with the total result of the voting in their several departments. Some were preceded by bands, some carried torches, some lanterns. In all, the men walked in long rows stretching across the breadth of the street, sweeping before them, or on to the pavement, all who did not care to join them. Being anxious to see where they went and what became of them, I joined the Eleventh Ward which had carried Lincoln by a large majority, and placing myself in the centre of a row of extremely noisy electors, I paraded a considerable portion of the town in this novel and exciting formation. Things went on smoothly enough barring a menacing storm of growls and hisses through which we had to pass at the democratic head quarters, until unfortunately in one of the narrowest streets of all, we met face to face the Eighth Ward which had inscribed upon its transparency an overwhelming majority for M'Clellan. I had been anticipating a crisis of this sort and wondering what would be the effect of it. But I need not have wondered. What could it be but an almighty row? The two bands broke off in the middle of their respective bars, and met in deadly conflict. The lanterns went out, the torches descended on the heads of the unwary, the democratic transparency got upset, and our's received a bullet through its centre. Some rushed forward to join the *mêlée*, some fled to the rear. Objecting to pistols, I took the latter course, and in the asylum of a friendly chemist's waited till the fray should cease. Two or three more pistol shots were exchanged, and some one was said to be wounded, but nobody seemed to take much notice of it, and in a short time the combatants had had enough of it and dispersed. Who was hit I never heard. The chemist appeared to think it nothing out of the common, and the papers said not a word about it ; but pistols are fair at any time in America, and *à fortiori* at an election. It was getting on in the small hours of the morning before I finally reached my hotel, and even then, and all night long, the streets were occupied by processions and crowds. What the actual result was it was utterly impossible to determine. Each side claimed a clear majority in each and every ward, and the state of uncertainty in which I went to bed was only aggravated by the morning papers, which proved, by incontestable evidence, that their respective parties had been magnificently triumphant.

However, I must say no more of the election. I will only add a word about my hotel, the Continental, the largest but one in the States. The prize Mammoth of these monstrous lodging-houses is that in the city of St. Louis, which has beds for half the State of Mississippi, and even then is so crowded that it has to litter down some of its visitors fifteen or

sixteen in a room. Fee, Fi, Fo, Fum, what a smell
of blood for the mosquitoes! Do not imagine that I
was subjected to the same infliction at the Continental. The house was preposterously full in consequence of the election, but I rebelled openly on being
shown into a dormitory with beds enough in it for a
hospital ward, and by turning on pretty strongly the
Civis Romanus tap, I succeeded in obtaining an Englishman's birthright, a room and castle to myself. In one
of my earliest letters I attempted to give you some
little idea of the hotel life of America, but I had not
then seen it in its grandest scale. All that I then
said of the size and stir and bustle of these leviathans
may be multiplied by ten, and that will still leave a
margin for due allowance for the microscopic properties
of an impulsive pen. The dining-halls, the corridors,
the ladies' boudoirs, the lifts and staircases themselves,
were at the Continental too tremendous in Egyptian-
like largeness and magnificence to give me any chance
of gaining credit for my story if I tell it you in detail.
Besides, what notion could you form of the house from
a dry list of facts and figures? What definite idea
have you ever got out of any statement of the superficial area of a continent, or the estimated distance of
a planet, out of any statistics indeed at all? Would
that I had John Leech's pencil to portray the scene
of gaiety and amusement that unrolls itself from morn
to eve within the walls of these hotels; or Charles

Dickens's pen to tell of the endless flow of life and labour, langour and love, that never ebbs from the seven o'clock breakfast to the midnight supper ; how the men bustle about the staircase, or loaf and lounge beside the counter in the hall ; how they sit and spit over their daily papers, and stand and spit about the bar ; how they sprawl on the chairs at the barber's shop, and smoke like chimneys everywhere ; how the women dress and sail about the corridors, how they feed at all the meals, how they talk politics and city markets in nasal notes an octave too high ; the jigs they play on the drawing-room piano, the instruments they play upon, and how they play them. Nothing can be more difficult of investigation than English life to a foreigner. Hedged round by all the impenetrable barriers of caste prejudices and cold reserve, and running in a hundred different grooves distinct and separate each from each, the English people in private life must seem to the inquiring stranger as unapproachable as the Tomb of Hebron ; but in the States it is far otherwise, and even if it were not, the hotels themselves would give the traveller an insight into the manners and customs of the country the like of which he could not get elsewhere. I do not for a moment wish you to infer that all America lives in hotels according to the popular notion of their mode of living entertained by us at home. But every hotel is a portrait in miniature of the city in which it stands.

In its halls, and dining-rooms, and around its bar, you may meet a representative of every class in the social scale. Merchants, lawyers, ministers of all creeds, soldiers, sailors, farmers, schoolmasters, can be met and talked to, and questioned, and joked with, as in their own private studies. Ladies, young, old, ugly, or pretty, can be seen and heard in their indoor manners. Boys and girls can be seen and wondered at in their utter ignorance of child-like playfulness. You can sit down at table with the Commander-in-chief and see him polish off his corn and iced water, and follow him down to the bar and scrutinise him over his cocktails. You may see the prettiest girl in the Union without her bonnet, and wonder how long it took her to do her hair; or hear the ugliest talk of stocks, and wonder where she learnt it all. You may stare at children at their meals going through the *carte* from top to bottom without parental interference or control, and marvel at their ever attaining a proper development under such a *régime* as that. You can get an insight —superficial it may be, but even that is veiled from you anywhere else—into social life of every grade, high, low, rich, poor, all ages and denominations, and study the habits of every class, and manners (when they have any). And all this without the slightest personal inconvenience, for you need do nothing but lounge about and keep your eyes and ears open, while the living diorama hurries on around you. And

the show, too, is cheap enough, little above the daily
expense of a stall at an ordinary theatre, and far more
instructing and amusing. English people think it
English to affect a dislike of these establishments, but
to a visitor they are everything. Frenchmen—and
they are very easily amused—say they die of *ennui* in
England, but no stranger need suffer from that disease
amongst the *ho*-tels of America.

And now for a few words about New York. This
great metropolis of all the world, of Irish, French,
Germans, Spaniards, Dutch, Indians, Chinese, of any
nation under the sun as much as of the Americans
themselves, has been talked and written of so much
that I can tell you little probably but what you have
heard or read already. Still you may possibly like to
know my private opinion of it, and so to begin with I
will take you down Broadway. Now if you have ever
met an American in England or on the Continent, you
will have been informed by him before you have had
five minutes' conversation with him, that no street in
the world is worth looking at after Broadway ; that
there is no thoroughfare in London, or Paris, or St.
Petersburg, half so wide, or one quarter so long, or one
tenth part so handsome, or one hundredth part so full
of life, and traffic, and business, and trade. If you
are talking of shops he will take the opportunity of
telling you that there is nothing like " our stores down

Broadway." If you observe upon the points of some passing beauty, he will "guess, sir, you've never seen our gals on Broadway." In short, Broadway licks *cre*-ation. It seems to form a common standard by which every Yankee measures everything he sees, length, breadth, height, magnitude, numbers, not to say rural scenery. He adopts it without inconsistency —so far as *he* sees—to comparisons of men and things in every phase of life; to estimates of the respective merits of town, or village, or mountain, or valley. I have heard an American crying down the only street of a little Italian village because its wretched hovels were not the marble hotels of Broadway. I have been told by another that the views on the Simplon Pass are not half so fine as Broadway. I know of another who guessed the great pyramid was not above twice as high as Stewart's stores in Broadway. If you ever travelled a journey with a Yankee and were not bored to death, or aggravated to madness, with his incessant harping on the superlative attractions of Broadway, then you must be a very angel at a long sermon, or be able to keep the great toe of your right foot more easy in its boot than I can. I do not object to a little of that conscientious patriotism which makes a man stretch his bow a harmless inch or two beyond the limits of statistical correctness in defence of his country when a foreigner's comparisons are becoming a little too odious; I have rather a respect for the

18

Englishman who tells the Parisian that the traffic in Fleet Street is so enormous that if you want to cross to the other side you must go right out into the country to do it; or for the Frenchman who tells the Londoner that it never by any chance rains, hails, or snows, or looks cloudy or uncomfortable in Paris; but for all that I cannot abide to hear a Yankee brag of Broadway; and what is more, I know nobody who can.

Well, I marched into this street of streets, expecting —I hardly know what. I thought, at least, it was twice as wide as Regent Street: it is exactly of the same width as New Oxford Street. I believed the houses were at least twice as high as those in the Canongate of Edinburgh: they are not so lofty as those in the Rue Rivoli. I imagined it was at least twice as long as Oxford Street: I suppose it is about half the length. But do not think I wish to disparage it. I only want to observe that the Yankees have no need to magnify and multiply into absurdities the actual merits of Broadway. Divide all they have said about it by five, or ten, or fifty, take it as it really is, and it remains, I honestly believe, one of the finest streets in the world. The Rue Rivoli is the only street I know that can at all compare with it; but that is a one-sided affair, of which the Tuilleries, perhaps, is the best part. But for one continuous line of pure street architecture— hotels, stores, and warehouses—I must admit, however

reluctantly, that Broadway has no equal. Stand at
the top of the two mile straight in which the street
stretches down to the ocean, and look down the long
vista of lofty, regular, solid buildings ; or see the clear
perspective of the street, as I saw it on the eve of the
great election, broken by flags and banners of every
hue, or spanned by waving canvas blazoned with
mottoes and devices ; descend the gay avenue of life
and colour, past the bright-fronted hotels of massive
white marble, past the colossal stores and warehouses,
many of them of white marble too, past the less pre-
tentious but noble houses of pale-brown freestone
that add warmth and colour to the architecture ; look
at the churches of the same stone, with their towers
perhaps ornamented with the Virginia creeper, or
buried in the shade of protecting maples ; glance
down the long streets that run right and left of the
main artery, built of the same warm-tinted stone that
peeps through the thick foliage of the trees which line
the pavement on either side ; peer into the stores and
the warehouse doorways, and the hotels and private
houses ; jostle with the crowd upon the side walks,
and watch the traffic in the centre of the road-way—
and then say if you know of any street in the world,
if you believe there be one, where you can find so
much magnificence of modern house architecture, such
regularity of outline, such grand uniformity, such
solidity of magnitude, so much lightness, and warmth,

and life, so much wealth, and dress, and colour, as make up the sensation picture of the view down Broadway.

But let us saunter down the street and take a passing glance at its details. My abode on my first visit to New York was at the Fifth Avenue Hotel, and we will start from its wide entrance—cross the handsome Square of which it is the chief ornament—pass down a small portion of Broadway into Union Square, still larger—through that, and down another portion of Broadway, consisting chiefly of private residences—by Grace Church, the fashionable church of the " Upper Ten " of New York—and enter upon the straight which will lead us down to Wall Street, and the battery, two miles distant. The atmosphere is clear as the skies of Italy—which, by-the-bye, I do not believe to be superior to many that I have seen at home, but the simile is the orthodox exemplification of the direct opposite of London smoke, and as such I use it—and in the smokeless distance we can see the sharp outline of the far-off steeple of Trinity Church, and the masts of the ships in the harbour beyond. On our way we pass the chief theatres, pre-eminent amongst which is Wallack's, and several which go by the name of " Gardens," a title that seems to suit any place of entertainment in or out of town alike; and before long we are at the St. Nicholas Hotel, a vast white marble edifice looking cool and comfortable nevertheless beneath the glare of the tropical sun by dint of the green Venetian shutters' with which its windows, like those of most of the houses, are furnished. Further on is the La Farge Hotel, a similar building, but less aristocratic, and on the other side more hotels, perhaps a step lower in the social scale; and so we come to Tiffany's store. Tiffany is the great jeweller, who has grown so fat on the extravagancies of the Shoddy which has been tossed to the surface in the convulsion of society caused by the war. Mr. Shoddy has spent his thousands, and Mrs. Shoddy her tens of thousands, in ornamentation of their respective persons until he and she can see in one another not merely a metaphorical jewel, but a perfect walking museum of heterogeneous gems and gildings. Prices are being asked and given for *articles de vertu* which would confound Harry Emanuel himself. But Tiffany is only one of the fatted calves. Ball and Black have gorged themselves as well upon the exorbitant demand for jewellery, and their store is almost opposite, so we will walk in and look at it. You can always do this. Premise, if such be your disposition, that you do not intend to buy anything, but merely have a curiosity to see, and you will find them ready enough to show. The building is large, lofty and handsome. The grand hall to which you enter from the street is decorated with taste and elegance, and fitted with numerous cases and cabinets of the choicest articles

in jewellery and plate. Above this hall is another
almost as large and rich in its contents, and above
that another still, equally worthy of a visit. In fact
the establishment is a perfect museum of modern gold-
smiths' and jewellers' work. But vast as is the scale
on which this business is conducted, it sinks into com-
parative insignificance by the side of Stewart's stores.
Stewart is the great " dry-goods merchant " of New
York, whose fame has long reached our shores. He
is, I suppose, next to the President, the best known
man in America. For " dry-goods " are a surer road
to fame than politics and legislation. His white
marble stores, one for the wholesale, the other for the
retail trade, would dwarf Marshall and Snelgrove's,
and Farmer and Rogers' into pigmies. We went over
one of them, ascending by the lift which carries up
the goods, through the successive tiers of show-rooms
and down the magnificent staircases which connect the
several flats, in utter amazement at the extent of the
area enclosed by the walls, and the business transacted
within them. But you must not linger here. A few
yards further on is the City Hall, in a meagre sort of
square, which is, I presume, as yet unfinished, as it
presents somewhat of the disreputable appearance of
the inclosure in Leicester Square ; and, as I saw it, was
rendered still more unsightly by a lot of ill-conditioned
recruiting booths, placarded with all sorts of announcements of the inconceivable advantages of serving in the

Federal army. Beside the hall are the law courts,
which were not in session, so that I had no opportunity of contrasting their method of doing business
with what I had seen at Chicago; but the courts
themselves were large, airy, and comfortable; as
superior to the dirty forcing-houses of Lincoln's Inn,
as is the great conservatory of Kew gardens to a
cottager's cucumber-frame. Opposite the square is
the noted Astor House, one of the chief hotels of
the city, with a crowd of idlers upon the steps of
its portico, pass it when you will, morning, noon, or
night. But over the way is Barnum's museum; and
how could I, who had heard this king of humbugs
lecture at Cambridge upon the theory of his trade,
resist a renewal of our acquaintance? The block of
houses in which he has located himself is all alive with
frescoes of zoological curiosities to attract the eye of
the passer by, and, judging by the external appearance
of the buildings, you might expect the size of the
museum to be, what he advertises it to be, "the
largest in the known world." But if you do, you do
not know Barnum. "Cultivate externals," has been
the motto of his life, and in accordance with this
principle he has possessed himself of an enormous
block, of which he occupies for his own purposes
the mere outside shell. The rest I suppose he
lets for warehouses. Consequently, on entering,
you find yourself, not in a spacious hall, or even

a decent room, but in a dirty narrow strip of gallery, a sort of boarding-school pie, nothing but crust, with a few dusty shelves on the inside, containing a mass of nothing higgledy piggledy, unimaginably mouldy and abominable. It is utterly impossible to make out any single article exhibited. Possibly that is so upon principle, for it is perfectly certain that Barnum's Museum would never contain any genuine wonder. The only thing I did decipher was a group of wax figures, playfully labelled "The Royal Family of England." Their style and execution was so atrociously vulgar and infamous, that I was half ashamed to be seen staring at them. But what is the use of being indignant at being hoaxed by Barnum. Did I not go into the trap with my eyes open ? Did I not, as I paid my 50 cents, know that I was throwing it away ? Then why storm at the imposition ? Fancy-bazaar prices are at times very aggravating ; but if a young lady gives you no change out of half a sovereign upon the purchase of a two-and-sixpenny tooth-brush, or charges you eighteen-pence for a strawberry which she has kissed, you have at least the consolation that she does not pocket the receipts herself. Now, I must say it is somewhat degrading to think that you are supporting an impostor who has lived for years upon the greenness of the public ; and yet the bare-faced impudence of the exhibition has a certain charm for admirers of original talent. And this, I suppose,

NEW YORK.   281

is what attracts the crowds who daily besiege Barnum's
doors ; and this, perhaps, is why they do not take offence
at the notice upon the empty aquarium, that "the
whale has unfortunately just died," and "the singing
fish has been inadvertently delayed," or at the placard
on the walls stating that "the giant is still confined
to his bed," and that "it is with the deepest regret
that Mr. Barnum informs the public, that the price of
admission has been necessarily raised on account of
the depreciation in the currency." However, I saw a
seal play an organ, and that was an exhibition of
cetaceous talent which, if you are anything of a natu-
ralist, you will probably think worth my entrance fee.

Well, Barnum's is a regular do, and having been
there long enough to get properly ashamed of ourselves
at being so done, we will pass on down Broadway,
which becomes more crowded with foot-passengers on
the side-walks, and blocked with carriages in the road-
way, as we advance towards the sea, and in a short
time we shall be in Wall Street. Wall Street, the
New World's "hell," where more fortunes have been
made and lost in one year of the last four than in centuries of the lives of other countries. It is an unimposing street, of no length, nor width, nor architectural
merit. Every other house is a broker's, with all sorts
of money, and its representative, paper, displayed
behind those diamond-patterned wire screens which
mark the *bureaux de change* in Fleet Street or the

Rue Rivoli.   The paper samples are as innumerable
and as various as the tribes of fungi, and many of
them much more mouldy and forlorn.   The issue is
so curious, and of such multiform diversity, that it
would be perfectly impossible to predicate of any paper
money what must be the *primâ facie* evidence of its
genuineness.   It may have a white face with a green
back, in fact be a "green-back," or a white face with
a red back, or be green, or red, or yellow, or brown,
or half a dozen colours all at once.   It may have represented on it a head of Washington, or Jefferson, or
Lincoln, or some other president, or a governor of a
state, or fifty others.   It may be issued anywhere, and
have been everywhere, and, consequently, be proportionally filthy.   You—who never see any but sums of
a decent amount represented by a paper currency, and,
perhaps, do not even know what an Irish one-pounder
may look, and smell, and feel like, after it has been
tolerably thumbed by our Irish population—can have
no conception of the abject state of unwholesomeness to
which a five-cent piece of paper money is reduced by a
few months' fingering in New York.   You may get a
handful of this degraded coinage in change for a
street-car fare, so utterly unsavory and abominable
that you will scarcely like to soil your fingers or your
pocket with its greasy nastiness.   It sticks to the
lining, to your fingers, to your watch; coils round
your pencil or your tooth-pick, or doubles itself into a

conglomerate of indistinguishable pulp. How much of this small paper is lost or rendered useless every day the banks alone can tell. The issue must be a clear gain to them. I should hardly suppose a tenth part of it would ever survive to claim a metal equivalent. Prussian and Austrian money is a mystery dark enough to perplex many a British tourist; Canadian coinage is almost as difficult of comprehension to any but a high wrangler; but none can be so diabolical as the present postage currency of the United States.

But I was speaking of Wall Street and its neighbourhood. And yet I do not know that I have much to say about it. If you want to see dirt and ungodliness, go to the bottom of it, and turn up Pearl Street. It is the oldest quarter of the town, where the Dutch built and traded years ago, ere ever the Yankee had a lo-cation and a name. But Dutch cleanliness has departed. Respectable merchants have all emigrated higher up into the city, and Pearl Street is left to moulder and putrefy in the hands of the poorer population, who, being chiefly Irish, hold the dirt as much too sacred to meddle with. Well, if you do not like Pearl Street and its smells, turn into the Bowery. You will find it little cleaner, but vastly more amusing. Fancy Tottenham Court Road half as wide again, and the houses in it twice as irregular; hang out all over the lower stories ten times as many carpets, clothes, tables, chairs, brooms, umbrellas, hats, and petticoats;

and spread about the pavement in everybody's way twenty times as many pots and pans and other articles of iron, glass and crockery; placard and advertise upon every vacant surface; turn the gin-palaces into "lager beer" saloons, with the exterior of a tenth-rate tap; do everything out of doors upon the side-walks, business, eating, drinking, and smoking, and do it all as if you had so much time on your hands that you hardly knew how to occupy it; and so you will have a tableau of the Bowery. If it was only narrow and full of filthy children, it would be much more like any of those curious old alleys of Genoa than a street of Anglo-Saxon householders.

But the sun is tropical, and so are the stenches, and we must leave St. Giles' for Belgravia. So we will cross to the Fifth Avenue. The contrast is complete. For a continuous array of handsome residences I suppose the Fifth Avenue is unrivalled. The material of which they are built is that beautiful brown freestone that I have mentioned as giving so much warmth to the aspect of Broadway. The maples that line the edge of the pavements cast a pleasant shade upon the lower windows, which are often surrounded by lovely creepers trained gracefully upon the walls. The doors are approached by flights of steps, for areas are unknown, and if they were not, the New York policeman is much too great a swell to carry on under-ground *liaisons* with the cook. If you want to see "a member of the force " really useful in his vocation, go and watch him at a dangerous corner of Broadway, and see the patronising air with which he conducts a nervous female through the crowd of hurrying vehicles. Was ever escort more tender of his charge than he, as he softly places his neatly gloved right hand behind the waist of his *protégée*, raising the while the natty whip which he carries in his left to warn the drivers that they must not pass until the lady be safe across. Do you wish for information about the locality of any house or street? Ask him, and note the business-like way in which he produces from his pocket a map of the city, and points out to you thereon the route which you ought to take. Not that it is a matter of much difficulty to find your way about New York. The streets are all so straight, and the system of numbering them is so extremely simple, that nothing but an excess of stupidity or " salmon " could cause you to lose yourself in the chief thoroughfares. Those which run parallel with the Hudson are called " avenues," those which intersect them rectangularly, " streets." The avenues and streets are all numbered, and the numbers are displayed upon the corner lamp-posts, so that by day or night they are equally legible. Arithmetical addresses do not look so well upon envelopes as our high-sounding voluminous descriptions, and Rotten Row loungers might object to being described upon their visiting cards as of " E.

27th and 3rd Av. 57A;" but a glance tells a New Yorker that the owner of the card occupies part of the corner house at the junction of East Twenty-seventh Street and Third Avenue, that his door is in the said street, and that 57A is his bell. Could the information be conveyed more briefly and effectively?

But we must follow the long line of vehicles that is making its way to the central park. Two miles or more of the beautiful Fifth Avenue have to be traversed before we reach the entrance gates. The park is still unfinished, but it promises to merit the loud praises which the New Yorkers prospectively bestow on it. It is far more like the Crystal Palace gardens at Sydenham than any of our city parks, for the ground is very uneven, broken into diminutive ravines and gullies, which have been skilfully taken advantage of by the landscape gardener who has superintended the work ; and there is a considerable surface of ornamental water, which winds about amongst the little vales ; and there are rocky islets on its bosom, and tasty bridges leading nowhere in particular, and waterfalls in unnatural situations, and fountains too, and orthodox grottoes, and terraces, and towers, and temples, and all the multitude of artificial details which we of the severer school think it scholar-like to denounce as " pandering to the vulgar eye," but which, for all our denunciations, are the most attractive incidents of a " people's garden." And now turn your eyes from the park to

the park's visitors. But look not for a Rotten Row,
nor anything the least like it. Americans do not
ride much for riding's sake, and when they do they
never rise in their stirrups, but attempt the cavalry
trot, and look very awkward and uncomfortable, and
very much as if they were of Mr. Briggs's mind to get
inside and pull the blinds down. Nor think to see
anything the least like our "drive." How can you
have anything resembling it without liveries and crests
and shields, and all the exploded emblems of a bloated
monarchy? How can you expect an erratic impulsive Yankee, volatile as a pea upon a hot plate, to
bear the tedium of crawling at a snail's place round a
pond in a "one-horse" vehicle of feudal times? No,
put him in his buggy, and then he is happy. With
wheels little broader than a halfpenny's edge, and a
pair that can trot their sixteen miles an hour, he can
bowl along down the Fifth Avenue, scamper round
the Central Park, dash off a few miles in the country
beyond, and another race round the park, shoot up the
Fifth Avenue like a telegram, and be at his door
again in less time than it takes us old fogies to think
about it. It will probably somewhat startle you to
see the buggies cutting about in every direction like
express trains at Clapham Junction, and you will most
likely be within an ace of being run down at least a
dozen times; but you will not find the park very interesting, and so I will take you back to the life

and bustle of the Fifth Avenue Hotel, and there our stroll through the town must end.

What I did in New York would fill a volume; but fear not, I am charitably-minded and shall spare you. There was always, as the Yankees say, "any quantity" to do. There was the Hudson to see, which we did, by making two delightful excursions up it, one about sixty miles to West Point, the great military school, which stands in one of the most lovely situations that can possibly be conceived—Heidelberg itself cannot be finer—and the other, about half-way there, to spend a happy day with a friend who lives in one of the pretty villages which skirt the river's banks, where we were regaled with native sherry, pure and excellent, as I never tasted sherry elsewhere. The scenery of the Hudson is magnificent. Steaming along by the rocky heights through which its waters wind, you might fancy yourself upon the Rhine, only that the colours of the autumn foliage are far too bright for European climates, and there are no quaint old fortresses upon the cliffs and promontories to cast down upon its sunny stream the shade of centuries ago. And how can I tell you of the endless diversion to be found in the streets themselves? Sometimes it was a procession of the famous fire-brigade, in their Garibaldi shirts and "dress" trousers, with their beautiful steam fire-engines burnished like mirrors, and decorated with

flowers and flags innumerable. Sometimes it was a
"turn out" of the representatives of some club or
union, in procession to the Cooper's Institute to hold
a meeting upon the presidential election, or simply
airing themselves and their banners. Sometimes it
was a string of regiments on their way from or to the
front. Sometimes a military funeral, solemn and
gorgeous; sometimes an Irish one, grotesque and ludicrous. Then there were the passengers on the side-
walks; goat-faced warriors in brigand hats; blue-
cheeked civilians behind enormous cigars; schoolgirls
with their bundles of books returning from their studies,
to which they had betaken themselves before the rest
of the world was astir, though the world of New York
is an early bird, and seven o'clock was the ladies'
breakfast hour in the boarding-house wherein I spent
a week of my visit. There were the omnibuses too
without conductors, where the driver took your fare or
not as you pleased to pay it through a hole in the roof
behind him; and the street-cars with their impudent
managers, always crammed and uncomfortable, for
there is no restriction as to the number of passengers,
and people hail them be they ever so full, and scramble
and cling on to the platform by which you ascend
behind, like bees clustering upon a bough.

Then there were the schools, of which we saw one,
perhaps the most interesting sight of any that I saw
in the States, where the pupils were all marched into

19

prayers, and out again into their separate class-rooms,
and wherever they had to move, to the music of piano-
fortes, upon the chords of which the orders were
sounded without word of command of any sort or kind.
I wish you could have seen for yourself the numbers
that were present in the great schoolroom, the marvellous discipline by which the fifteen hundred boys
and girls were kept in order, without any other system
of punishment for misbehaviour than refusal of per-
mission to attend the school.   I should like to tell
you how the principal astonished me by this statement
of their corrective system, and how I amused him by
declaring that you might as well try to tame a tiger
as think of keeping in order a room-full of fifteen hundred English scholars by the notes of a piano, with none
but the negative punishment for misconduct of a limited
banishment from study.   But I have before observed
upon the marked difference of nature between the
children of the two continents, and certain it is that
there is something in the American climate and constitution which smothers the natural ebullitions of fun
and frolic and childlike playfulness that are the charm
of an English child.   The very kittens in the States
are dull and grave as stoics.   Yet I dare say this stoical
demeanour of the Yankee children conduces to the
success of their educational system, which all the world
knows, is as perfect as popular education ever was.

And now I must say good-bye to America.   Though

my subject is not exhausted, your patience must be, and so I will bring my story to a close. How I spent my time on the voyage home, and how it blew head-winds for the first five of the twelve days we were out, and how it rained for the next three, and how slow it was during the other four and everybody longed for the sight of land, and how they brightened up as the old " Kangaroo " neared it, till they got quite boisterous at the first glimpse of the Irish coast, matters little. Sea voyages are all alike, except that some are more unpleasant than others, and having given you a voluminous extract ·from the log of my outward trip, I dare not inflict upon you another. There never is anything to do at sea but smoke, flirt, eat, or read novels ; and you cannot be for ever at these without finding a sad monotony in the amuse-ment. Besides, if you have not a boatswain's stomach, it takes you pretty nearly half one of these Atlantic voyages to get up an appetite for any of these pur-suits. For it is pretty sure to blow, or rain, or do both ; and then you have to swelter and pant below in the stifling fustiness of the saloon, with all the windows screwed down, and perhaps a five-days-old smell of greasy dinner and engine-oil and sick passengers, an odour to which the monkey-house in the Zoological is as Rimmell's Ess Bouquet ; or you retire to your cabin only to find it a condensed smelling-box of these vapours, and your cabin com-

panion overcome in the middle of it. And then the
torture of the toilette, the bumps your head gets
against the basin or the wall, the abject helplessness
in which you are kept involuntarily dancing about
like a Perfect Cure, with your arms and knees at all
sorts of drunken angles, like a puppet in a Pantochini-
box ; and, worst of all, the agonies of a night with
a heavy swell on, the inane way in which you tumble
about the ledge whereon you try to lie, the wisps into
which your sheets, no bigger than towels, roll themselves under your labours, the games your portmanteau
has with your friend's hat-box upon the floor, the
playful gambols of the passengers' boots with the
books in the saloon, the appalling smashes amongst
the crockery in the steward's cabin—all these are incidents of an ocean trip which have been food for
many a graphic pen, and all of us know more or less
of their miseries. Then, if it should be fine, what are
you to do ? There are two or three extremely innocent pastimes, invented by the fertile brain of some
muscular Christian in alarm at the bad condition to
which he must be reduced by the deprivation of all
bodily exercise beyond the ten-yard-constitutional he
could get by doubling and redoubling like a tethered
sentry. But they are all peculiarly slow. Sea-quoits,
which consists in laying hoops in a pail, reduces itself
to a certainty, and becomes very mild. Shuffle-board
is perhaps still milder. Follow-the-leader, which the

emigrants play, is simply childish; and gymnastic evolutions about the rigging entail heavy fines, and the prospect of being lashed up by the sailors until payment.

How dull and quarrelsome everybody got during the last half of the passage, how they longed for the sight of land, and how they brightened up on nearing it, and how envious the Liverpool passengers were of me because I was going to disembark at Queenstown, I leave you to imagine. There my travels were practically at an end. How pretty I thought the harbour of Queenstown, how green and homely the Emerald Isle, how strange it was to come from a country where I had seen scarce half a dozen ill-clad people to a place where everybody seemed to be in the last stage of filth and pauperism, how the women all looked as if they had clothed themselves in relics of tattered attic carpets, and the men always had the seats of their trousers patched into the backs of their coats, and no buttons upon their garments where they should be, and holes in them unmistakable where they should not—all this and more I need not tell, though I am loth to lay aside my pen, pleasant as it is, and always must be, to sit and scribble about what one has seen and heard, as if one were a perfect Gulliver of travel, and had visited scenes in unknown lands where no human foot had ever trod. But things are seen by different eyes in very different and altered aspects, and stories of things described as seen may constantly present some new feature. I have tried to tell you what I have seen exactly as each object impressed me at the moment I saw it, and this must be my excuse for much that second thoughts might have omitted. I cannot hope to have interested you one half as much as I have amused myself. But scribbling is the tourist's safety-valve, whereby he can let off with less annoyance to his friends what is apt to become tedious in conversation. Bacon, I know, has counselled the traveller to " be rather advised in his answers than forward to tell stories ;" but he has closed his advice with another maxim, in the spirit of which you must consider me to have acted in the inditing of these letters—" When a traveller returneth home, let him not leave the countries where he hath travelled altogether behind him."

THE END.

PRINTED BY J. E. ADLARD, BARTHOLOMEW CLOSE.

www.ingramcontent.com/pod-product-compliance
Lightning Source LLC
Chambersburg PA
CBHW031410270326
41929CB00010BA/1404